Xamarin Mobile Application Development for Android

Learn to develop full featured Android apps using your existing C# skills with Xamarin.Android

Mark Reynolds

PUBLISHING

BIRMINGHAM - MUMBAI

Xamarin Mobile Application Development for Android

First published: January 2014

Production Reference: 1080114

Published by Packt Publishing Ltd.
Livery Place
35 Livery Street
Birmingham B3 2PB, UK.

ISBN 978-1-78355-916-9

www.packtpub.com

Cover Image by Gagandeep Sharma (er.gagansharma@gmail.com)

Credits

Author
Mark Reynolds

Reviewers
Carlo Wahlstedt
Edward Wilde

Acquisition Editors
Meeta Rajani
Martin Bell

Commissioning Editor
Shaon Basu

Technical Editors
Novina Kewalramani
Menza Mathew
Pratik More

Copy Editors
Dipti Kapadia
Kirti Pai

Project Coordinator
Sherin Padayatty

Proofreader
Amy Johnson

Indexer
Mehreen Deshmukh

Graphics
Ronak Dhruv
Abhinash Sahu

Production Coordinator
Komal Ramchandani

Cover Work
Komal Ramchandani

About the Author

Mark Reynolds is a software enthusiast who has worked in the industry for nearly 30 years. He began his career with Electronic Data Systems, building and supporting systems for the manufacturing sector. Over the years, he has worked with companies ranging in size from startups to Fortune 500 across a diverse set of industries including manufacturing, entertainment, financial services, government, and telecom. In 1993, Mark started a consulting practice focused on delivering training and mentoring services in the areas of software architecture, design, and implementation. With the rise of mobile computing, Mark has returned to what he loves the most, designing, developing, and delivering software solutions, now focusing in the mobile computing space. He continues his private consulting practice based in Allen, TX, where he also resides with his wife and son.

Mark works as an independent consultant through his own private consulting practice (RSEG) based in Allen, TX, a community located north of Dallas. You can find out more about the services he offers from his website, `rseg.net`.

I would like to say thank you to my wonderful, God-given wife for all her encouragement and support, to my wonderful, God-given son for his creative inspiration, to all my customers who fund my interest in mobile computing, and to all the supporting staff and reviewers associated with Packt Publishing—they've had a big impact on the content and usability of this book.

About the Reviewers

Carlo Wahlstedt, a husband and a follower of Jesus, is a lover of technology. Since graduating from Berea College, he's held jobs dealing with hardware testing, and software designing. He's been focusing on software in some capacity since 2006 but feels that to be a good software engineer, you need to understand many aspects of hardware as well. His software experience ranges across many technologies, but he has the most experience on the Microsoft stack. He's been a self-proclaimed geek since 1990 and an Android lover since 2007.

Edward Wilde started his programming adventure with the BBC Micro Model B at the tender age of seven. He entered the software industry commercially in 1997, when he founded a web consultancy with his brother, Andrew. He has a keen interest in all the aspects of software development, ranging from web development to low latency, multithreaded, financial applications.

www.PacktPub.com

Support files, eBooks, discount offers and more

You might want to visit www.PacktPub.com for support files and downloads related to your book.

Did you know that Packt offers eBook versions of every book published, with PDF and ePub files available? You can upgrade to the eBook version at www.PacktPub.com and as a print book customer, you are entitled to a discount on the eBook copy. Get in touch with us at service@packtpub.com for more details.

At www.PacktPub.com, you can also read a collection of free technical articles, sign up for a range of free newsletters and receive exclusive discounts and offers on Packt books and eBooks.

http://PacktLib.PacktPub.com

Do you need instant solutions to your IT questions? PacktLib is Packt"s online digital book library. Here, you can access, read and search across Packt"s entire library of books.

Why Subscribe?

- Fully searchable across every book published by Packt
- Copy and paste, print and bookmark content
- On demand and accessible via web browser

Free Access for Packt account holders

If you have an account with Packt at www.PacktPub.com, you can use this to access PacktLib today and view nine entirely free books. Simply use your login credentials for immediate access.

Table of Contents

Preface

In the fall of 2013, when Packt Publishing first approached me about writing this book, it was a no brainer; of course I would. Why? Why not? A book about mobile development using Xamarin.Android; I'm in! I have to admit, I didn't start here; it was a journey for me.

I've always been keen on cross-platform development environments. I'm not really fond of learning new ways to do the same thing using a different syntax unless there is significant productivity gains associated with it. Ten years ago, the foregone conclusion for most was that cross-platform development belonged to Java; I was on board with that. Had anyone told me that in 2013, with the rise of mobile computing, I would be doing all my cross-platform mobile development with C#, I would have laughed. So, how did I get here?

It started in 2010. I was struggling with Objective-C, trying to get an iOS prototype up and running. One day, I described the prototype to a colleague, Ed Tighe. Ed suggested that I look into MonoTouch. As I recall, the conversation went something as follows:

Me: MonoTouch? What is that?

Ed: A Mono-based development environment for iOS.

Me: Mono… you mean Mono; as in the open source cross-platform C# thing?

Ed: That's the one.

Me: Is that still around? Who would trust Mono with a mission critical solution? What's the likelihood they will be around in four to five years?

Sometimes Ed says funny things; I chalked this one up to that. I was completely dismissive of the idea. It wasn't that I didn't respect what the Mono project and contributors had achieved; it was more about the overriding belief that at some point Microsoft would decide Mono did not need to exist and would work against its continued progress. I also had serious reservations about whether support and long term commercial viability was there. However, the one thing Mono had in its favor was a mass of C# developers that could adopt their platform with minimal investment.

In early 2012, I was approached by Andy LaBrunda, VP of IT, for a telecom-based on Guam, about developing mobile apps for prepaid customers. I knew they were a .NET shop and were looking for both iOS and Android apps with the possibility of a Windows Phone app in the future. I also knew they had a relatively small set of developers, who would be tasked with supporting the apps, and they already knew C#, .NET, and rich client development using WPF.

With all this in mind, it only made sense to consider MonoTouch and Mono for Android. The GTA staff would not have to learn Objective-C and Java, and we would achieve some level of reuse between the two apps, so we framed up a small proof of concept effort, the goal being to build two apps with only a few screens, hook the apps up to RESTful services, and share some code between the apps. As always, when I get to play with new technology, I am excited so I approached this effort with great optimism. I wasn't disappointed; the Xamarin products delivered on everything we set out to prove. I was sold and have never looked back. We built out the two prepaid apps and moved on to build out two postpaid apps.

Since then, I have spent significant time and energy building out my Xamarin practice, including writing this book. I've also taken what we learned at GTA and I'm now working with a company in the Dallas area in the entertainment industry building customer facing apps. With the recent strengthening of the relationship between Xamarin and Microsoft, I believe that Mono and the Xamarin product line have a bright future.

The idea behind this book was to bring the base set of knowledge required to build Android apps with Xamarin.Android together in a convenient, concise, productive format that could be used by those looking to get started with the product. I have always been a fan of learning experiences structured around building solutions, or examples, incrementally throughout the book so that the approach we settled on for this book. We begin with two chapters of general Android and Xamarin architecture and then step through building a Point of Interest app that demonstrates the basics of building Android apps, including some of the more interesting features such as integration with location services, the map app, and the camera app. Our goal has been to provide you with a productive learning experience; I hope we have achieved that and I thank you for taking the time to read it.

Oh! And one more thing on this topic; Ed, you were right.

What this book covers

Chapter 1, The Anatomy of an Android App, provides an overview of the Android platform and what Android apps are composed of.

Chapter 2, Xamarin.Android Architecture, describes the use of Mono, describes how Mono and the Dalvik runtime work together, and the Android platform coexist and allow developers to build Android apps using C#.

Chapter 3, Creating the Points of Interest App, walks the reader through creating a new app and running the app within the Android emulator.

Chapter 4, Creating a Data Storage Mechanism, presents a number of options for storing data on an Android device and steps the reader through creating a JSON-based solution.

Chapter 5, Adding a List View, describes Android's AdapterView architecture and steps the reader through using ListView and creating a custom adapter.

Chapter 6, Adding a Detail View, walks the reader through creating a detail view to view a point of interest, adding navigation from the list view, and adding actions for saving and deleting information.

Chapter 7, Making POIApp Location Aware, presents the various options that developers have to make their apps location aware and walks the reader through adding logic to determine a device's location and the address of a location, and displaying a location within the map app.

Chapter 8, Adding Camera App Integration, presents the various options that developers have to add integration with the device camera and walks the reader through adding integration with camera apps on device.

Chapter 9, Deploying Your App, discusses the various options for distributing Android apps and walks the reader through preparing a Xamarin.Android app for distribution.

What you need for this book

All of the examples in this book can be completed using a 30-day trial version of Xamarin.Android. The examples were developed using Windows 7, Xamarin Studio 4.0.13, and Xamarin.Android 4.8.3 (Trial Edition). Any later versions should work fine as long as they are valid Xamarin configurations. Check the Xamarin website for specifics.

Xamarin.Android can also be used in other configurations. Xamarin Studio can also be used in OS X. Visual Studio 2012 and the Xamarin plugin can be used instead of Xamarin Studio. Using a different configuration from what was used in developing the example may result in slight variations in the screens or steps described in the book.

To run the example app on an actual device, you will need a device running Android 4.1 or advanced.

Who this book is for

This book is great for C# developers that have a desire to develop Android apps using their existing skill sets. It's assumed that you have a good working knowledge of C#, .NET, and object-oriented software development. Familiarity with rich client technologies such as WPF or Silverlight is also helpful but not required.

Conventions

In this book, you will find a number of styles of text that distinguish between different kinds of information. Here are some examples of these styles and an explanation of their meaning.

Code words in text are shown as follows: "An Android package is created as the result of compiling an Android app and is an archive file with a `.apk` extension."

A block of code is set as follows:

```xml
<?xml version="1.0" encoding="utf-8"?>
<LinearLayout xmlns:android="http://schemas.android.com/apk/res/
android"
  android:orientation="vertical"
  android:layout_width="fill_parent"
  android:layout_height="fill_parent">
  <TextView
    android:text="Enter Search Criteria"
    android:layout_width="fill_parent"
    android:layout_height="wrap_content"
    android:id="@+id/searchCriteriaTextView" />
  <Button
    android:text="Search"
    android:layout_width="fill_parent"
```

```
            android:layout_height="wrap_content"
            android:id="@+id/searchButton" />
    </LinearLayout>
```

New terms and **important words** are shown in bold. Words that you see on the screen, in menus or dialog boxes for example, appear in the text like this: "Click through the first two welcome pages and the agreement page until you come to the **Product selection** page."

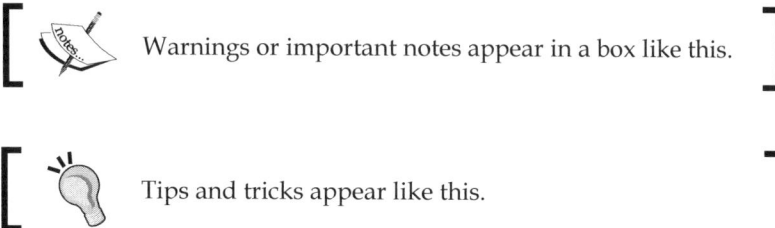

Warnings or important notes appear in a box like this.

Tips and tricks appear like this.

Reader feedback

Feedback from our readers is always welcome. Let us know what you think about this book—what you liked or may have disliked. Reader feedback is important for us to develop titles that you really get the most out of.

To send us general feedback, simply send an e-mail to feedback@packtpub.com, and mention the book title through the subject of your message.

If there is a topic that you have expertise in and you are interested in either writing or contributing to a book, see our author guide on www.packtpub.com/authors.

Customer support

Now that you are the proud owner of a Packt book, we have a number of things to help you to get the most from your purchase.

Downloading the example code

You can download the example code files for all Packt books you have purchased from your account at http://www.packtpub.com. If you purchased this book elsewhere, you can visit http://www.packtpub.com/support and register to have the files e-mailed directly to you.

Errata

Although we have taken every care to ensure the accuracy of our content, mistakes do happen. If you find a mistake in one of our books—maybe a mistake in the text or the code—we would be grateful if you would report this to us. By doing so, you can save other readers from frustration and help us improve subsequent versions of this book. If you find any errata, please report them by visiting http://www.packtpub.com/support, selecting your book, clicking on the **errata submission form** link, and entering the details of your errata. Once your errata are verified, your submission will be accepted and the errata will be uploaded to our website, or added to any list of existing errata, under the Errata section of that title.

Piracy

Piracy of copyright material on the Internet is an ongoing problem across all media. At Packt, we take the protection of our copyright and licenses very seriously. If you come across any illegal copies of our works, in any form, on the Internet, please provide us with the location address or website name immediately so that we can pursue a remedy.

Please contact us at copyright@packtpub.com with a link to the suspected pirated material.

We appreciate your help in protecting our authors, and our ability to bring you valuable content.

Questions

You can contact us at questions@packtpub.com if you are having a problem with any aspect of the book, and we will do our best to address it.

1
The Anatomy of an Android App

While most of this book will be focused on learning how to develop Android apps using C# and Xamarin.Android, we will start with a more general discussion of Android. What is Android? How does Android facilitate the task of creating great mobile apps? *The Anatomy of an Android App* will help to answer these questions by providing a base-level understanding of the following topics:

- The Android platform
- Android applications (Building Blocks)

The Android platform

The Android platform has been one of the most successful platforms developed in recent years and provides developers with many services and features required to create rich mobile applications. The following diagram provides a high-level view of how the Android platform is organized, and the subsequent sections provide a brief description of each major component:

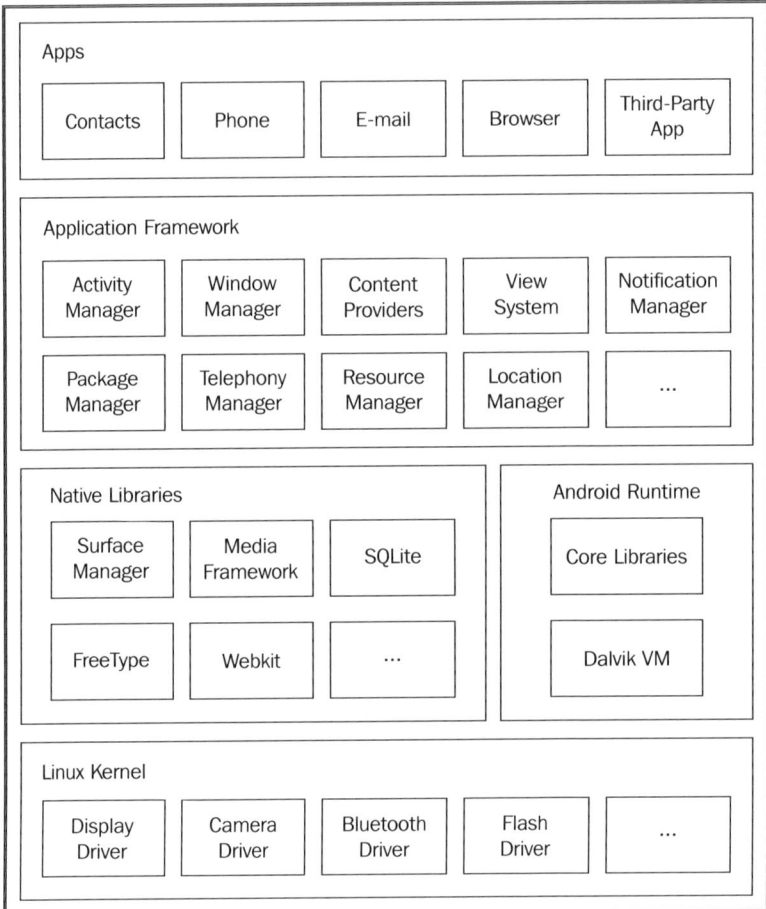

Linux

Android is a Linux-based operating system designed primarily for mobile devices such as smartphones and tablets. The latest versions of Android are based on Linux kernel Version 3.x (Version 2.6 for versions prior to Android 4.0).

Native libraries

Android is delivered with a set of native libraries written in C/C++, which provide various types of services. These libraries predominantly come from the open source community.

The Android runtime

Android apps run within the **Dalvik Virtual Machine (Dalvik VM)**, which is similar to a Java VM but has been optimized for devices with limited memory and processing capacity.

Android apps are initially compiled to the Java byte code using the Java compiler, but they have an additional compilation step that transforms the Java byte code to the Dalvik byte code, suitable to run within the Dalvik VM.

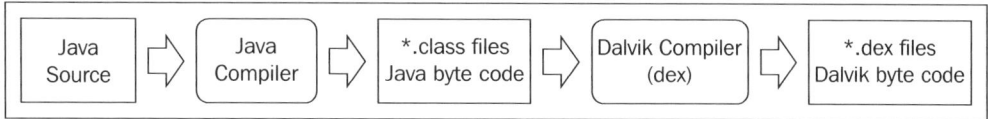

Dalvik is delivered with the Android core libraries. These libraries do not align with a specific Java platform (JSE, JEE, or JME) but rather act as a hybrid platform most closely aligned with JSE, minus the user interface-focused components AWT and Swing. The **Android Application Framework (AAF)** provides an alternate means of creating user interfaces.

The Application Framework

The Application Framework is the part of the Android platform, most familiar to developers. It is delivered as a set of Java libraries and allows you to build user interfaces, interact with device capabilities such as the camera or location services, load and work with various types of application resources, and perform many more useful tasks.

Applications

At the top of the stack sits the humble application, the component that actually delivers value to the user. Android comes with a set of applications that provide base functionality such as managing contacts, using the phone, checking email, and browsing the Web. The key to Android's success is the vast array of third-party applications that can be installed, which allow users to do things such as stream live sports' events, edit a movie captured on the phone, interact with friends through their favorite social media site, and much more.

The Android packages (.apk)

Applications are delivered for installation in an Android package format. An Android package is created as the result of compiling an Android app and is an archive file with a .apk extension. An Android package contains all of the code and the supporting files required to run a single application including the following:

- Dalvik executables (*.dex files)
- Resources
- Native libraries
- The application manifest

Android packages can be installed directly via e-mails, URLs, or memory cards. They can also be installed indirectly through app stores such as Google Play.

The application manifest

All Android applications have a manifest file (AndroidManifest.xml) that tells the Android platform everything it needs to know to successfully run the application, including the following:

- Minimum API Level required by the application
- Hardware/software features used or required by the application
- Permissions required by the application
- The initial screen (Android activity) to start with when the application is launched
- Libraries, other than AAF, required by the application
- And so on

Versions of Android

Identifying the version of the Android platform can be somewhat confusing; there is a version number, API level, and nickname, and these are sometimes used interchangeably.

The version number represents a release of the platform. Sometimes, a new release is created to deliver new capabilities, while sometimes it is created to fix bugs.

The API level represents a set of capabilities. As the API level increases, new capabilities are delivered to the developer.

The following table lists the versions of the platform in the reverse chronological order:

Platform version	API level	Nickname	Released
4.4	19	KitKat	10/31/2013
4.3	18	Jelly Bean	07/24/2013
4.2, 4.22	17		11/13/2012
4.1, 4.11	16		07/09/2012
4.0.3, 4.0.4	15	Ice Cream Sandwich	12/16/2011
4.0, 4.01, 4.02	14		10/19/2011
3.2	13	Honeycomb	07/15/2011
3.1.x	12		05/10/2011
3.0.x	11		02/22/2011
2.3.3, 2.3.4	10	Gingerbread	02/02/2011
2.3, 2.3.1, 2.3.2	9		12/06/2010
2.2.x	8	Froyo	05/20/2010
2.1.x	7	Éclair	01/12/2010
2.0.1	6		12/03/2009
2.0	5		10/26/2009
1.6	4	Donut	09/15/2009

The Android applications

Now, let's spend some time discussing applications—those things we write that provide value to the user. Android applications are made up of various types of classes and resources. The following sections describe the different types of classes or building blocks that an application can be composed of.

Activities

One of the most fundamental parts of an Android application is an activity. An activity provides a single function that a user can perform with an application such as list contacts, enter new contact, and display location(s) on a map. A single application is composed of many activities.

A user interacts with an activity through one or more Views, which are described later in this chapter. If you are familiar with the Model-View-Controller pattern, you would have noticed that activities fulfill the role of the Controller.

The life cycle of an activity

Activities have a well-defined life cycle that can be described in terms of states, transitions, and events. The following diagram provides a graphical view of the life cycle of an activity:

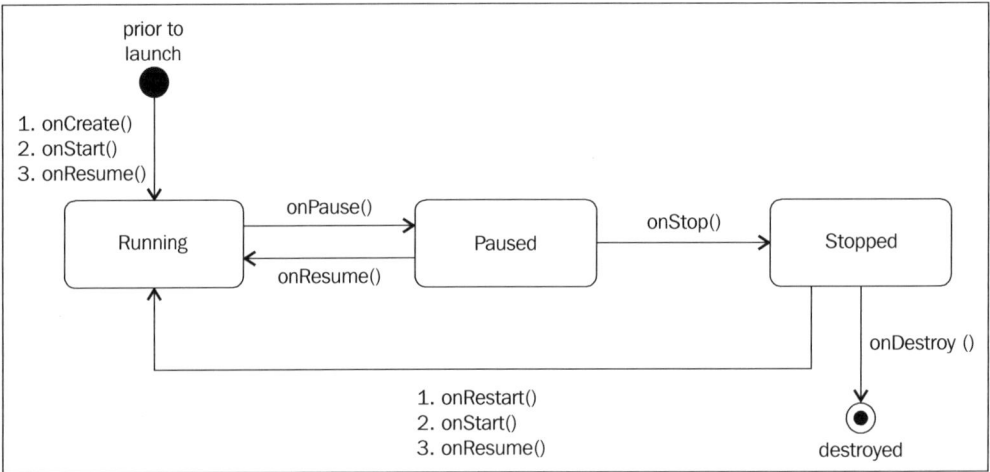

The states of an activity

The states depicted in the previous diagram are derived, meaning there is no "State" variable on an activity that explicitly identifies one of these states, but the state is implied and useful for discussion. The following table describes the behavior of an activity based on its state:

State	Description
Running	The activity has been created and initialized, and is visible and available to the user for interaction.
Paused	The activity view is being partially blocked by another activity.
Stopped	The activity is no longer visible to the user, The activity has not been destroyed, and state is retained but it is placed in the background and no processing is allowed.

The events of an activity

During the transition between states, a series of events are called on the activity. These events provide developers a platform for various types of processing.

Event	Called	Typical processing
onCreate	When an activity is created, generally from a user choosing to start the app	• Create Views • Initialize variables • Allocate long-lived resources
onStart	After onCreate or onRestart and right before an activity becomes visible to the user	• Allocate resources
onResume	Before an activity is ready to start interacting with a user	• Initialize UI widgets for viewing • Starting animations or videos • Start listening for GPS updates
onPause	When an activity's view has become partially blocked and is not the focus of input	• Commit unsaved updates • Pause animations or videos • Stop listening for GPS updates
onStop	When an activity's view is no longer visible to the user	• Release resources
onRestart	An activity is being placed back in the foreground, generally because the user has selected the back button	• Allocate resources
onDestroy	Before the activity is destroyed	• Cleanup resources that may have been allocated in onCreate

Something that is not obvious to developers new to Android is the way the framework deals with device orientation changes. By default, when the orientation of a device is changed from portrait to landscape, Android destroys and recreates existing activities to help ensure that the most appropriate layout is used. Unless this behavior is planned for, it can be very disruptive to processing. If needed, this behavior can be overridden and activities can be retained. We will discuss special considerations in dealing with state and other processing concerns related to this topic in *Chapter 7, Making POIApp Location Aware*.

Services

Services are components that run in the background to perform long-running operations with no direct user interface. Services may load data into a cache, play music, or perform some other type of processing, while a user interacts with other activities uninterrupted.

Content providers

Content providers manage access to a central repository of data such as contacts. A content provider is a part of an application, which usually provides a user interface to manage its data. A standard interface is also provided, which allows other applications to access its repository.

Broadcast receivers

Broadcast receivers are components that perform some type of processing in response to system-wide broadcasts. Broadcasts are generally initiated by the system for events such as low battery, taking a picture, or turning on Bluetooth. Applications may also choose to send broadcasts; a content provider might send a broadcast when data, such as a contact, has been updated. While broadcast receivers do not have a user interface, they may indirectly cause updates to a status.

Views and ViewGroups

Everything that you see in an Android app is a View; buttons, labels, text boxes, and radio buttons are all examples of Views. Views are organized in a hierarchy using various types of ViewGroups. A ViewGroup is a special kind of View which is used to arrange (layout) other Views on the screen.

Declarative versus programmatic View creation

Views and ViewGroups can be created using two different methods, programmatically or declaratively. When using a programmatic approach, a developer makes API calls to create and position each individual View in the UI. When using a declarative approach, a developer creates XML layout files that specify how Views should be arranged. The declarative method enjoys several advantages stated as follows:

- Provides better separation of the visual design of an application from the processing logic
- Allows multiple layouts to be created to support multiple devices or device configurations with a single code base
- Development tools, such as Android Studio and the Android plugin for Eclipse, allow you to view the user interface as you build it, without needing to compile and execute your application after each change

While I prefer the declarative method for most things, I have found that, in practice, some combination of programmatic and declarative methods are often required.

User interface widgets

Android provides a comprehensive set of user interface widgets that can be used to build a rich user experience. All of these widgets are subtypes of View and can be organized into sophisticated layouts using various types of ViewGroups. All of the user interface widgets can be found in the `android.widget` package within the Application Framework.

Common layouts

The Application Framework has a number of subclasses of `ViewGroup`, each of which provides a unique and useful way of organizing content.

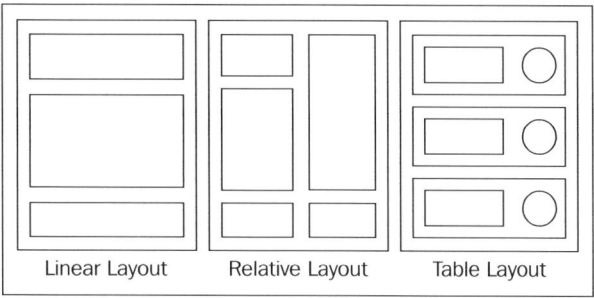

Linear Layout   Relative Layout   Table Layout

The previous diagram depicts a few of the more common layouts, each of which can be used for specific needs.

Layout	Description	Scenario
Linear layout	Organizes its children into a single horizontal or vertical row and creates a scrollbar when required.	Use when a widget positions flow horizontally or vertically.
Relative layout	Organizes child objects relative to each other or to the parent.	Use when widget positions can best be described in relationship to another widget (to the left of) or the boundary area of the parent (right side, centered).
Table layout	Organizes its children into rows and columns.	Use when widget positions would naturally fit into rows and columns. Great when multiple columns of entry and labels are needed.

For complex layout scenarios, Android allows layouts to be nested. Deeply nested layouts can impact performance and should be avoided if possible.

Adapter layouts

For layouts that are driven by a dynamic data source, the Application Framework has a set of classes derived from `AdapterView`.

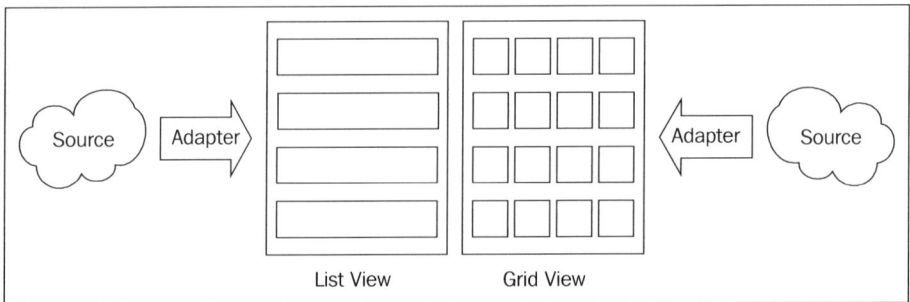

List View   Grid View

The previous diagram depicts two of the most common adapter layouts.

- **List View**: Organizes content from the data source into a scrolling single column list
- **Grid View**: Organizes content from the data source into a grid of columns and rows

XML layout files

To create a UI using a declarative method, Android provides an XML vocabulary with tags that define the various types of elements that can compose a View. The concept behind Android XML layout files is very similar to the way HTML tags are used to define web pages or Microsoft's XAML tags are used to define **WPF (Windows Presentation Foundation)** user interfaces. The following example shows a simple View using a linear layout and containing a search entry field and search button:

```
<?xml version="1.0" encoding="utf-8"?>
<LinearLayout xmlns:android="http://schemas.android.com/apk
/res/android"
  android:orientation="vertical"
  android:layout_width="fill_parent"
  android:layout_height="fill_parent">
  <TextView
    android:text="Enter Search Criteria"
    android:layout_width="fill_parent"
    android:layout_height="wrap_content"
    android:id="@+id/searchCriteriaTextView" />
    <Button
      android:text="Search"
      android:layout_width="fill_parent"
      android:layout_height="wrap_content"
      android:id="@+id/searchButton" />
</LinearLayout>
```

Element and attribute names

Care has been taken to aligning the names for elements and attributes in the XML vocabulary with class and method names from the Application Framework. In the previous example, the element names LinearLayout, TextView, and Button correspond to class names in the Application Framework. Likewise, in the Button element, the android:text attribute corresponds to the setText() setter on the Button class.

IDs

Each View can have a unique integer ID associated with it and can be used to reference the View from within an application's code. In the XML file, the ID is specified as a user friendly text name. For example, consider the following line of code:

```
android:id="@+id/searchButton"
```

In this example, the @ operator tells the parser that it should treat the remainder of the string as an ID resource; the + symbol tells the parser that this is a new resource name that should be added to the resource file, R.java. The resource file defines integer constants that can be used to reference resources.

Using XML layouts from activities

XML layouts can easily be loaded by an application at runtime. This task is generally performed from within the onCreate() method of an activity using the setContentView() method. For example, consider the following line of code:

```
setContentView(R.layout.main);
```

Intents

Intents are messages that can be sent to the various types of components in an Android App in order to request some type of action to be performed. Intents may be used to accomplish any of the following:

1. Start an activity with the option of receiving a result.
2. Start or stop a service.
3. Notify the component of conditions like low battery or time zone change.
4. Request an action from another app, such as request the map app to display a location or request that the camera app take a picture and save it.

Resources

Creating an Android application involves more than simply writing code. A rich mobile app requires things such as images, audio files, animations, menus, and style, just to name a few. The Application Framework provides APIs that can be used to load and utilize the various types of resources with your Android apps.

Downloading the example code

You can download the example code files for all Packt books you have purchased from your account at http://www.packtpub.com. If you purchased this book elsewhere, you can visit http://www.packtpub.com/support and register to have the files e-mailed directly to you.

The R.java file

Resources are generally referenced from within an application using an integer constant that is automatically assigned when the resource is added to the project and compiled. These constants are placed in a Java source file named `R.java`. The following example shows the `R.java` class from a simple application:

```java
public final class R {
  public static final class attr {
  }
  public static final class drawable {
    public static final int icon=0x7f020000;
  }
  public static final class id {
    public static final int myButton=0x7f050000;
    public static final int searchButton=0x7f050002;
    public static final int searchCriteriaTextView=0x7f050001;
  }
  public static final class layout {
    public static final int main=0x7f030000;
    public static final int search=0x7f030001;
  }
  public static final class string {
    public static final int app_name=0x7f040001;
    public static final int hello=0x7f040000;
  }
}
```

Summary

In this chapter, we have tried to provide a concise and adequate description of the Android platform and the application's building blocks. In the next chapter, we will turn our attention to Xamarin.Android and the facilities it provides to allow for Android development with .NET and C#.

Xamarin.Android Architecture

Now that we have an understanding of the Android platform, let's talk about Xamarin. In this chapter, we will look at the architecture of Xamarin.Android and how it facilitates the development of Android apps using C# and .NET. This chapter covers the following topics:

- The benefits and drawbacks of adopting Xamarin.Android
- What is Mono?
- Mono and Dalvik side by side (peer objects)
- Xamarin.Android binding libraries
- IDE choices

Xamarin is a company which provides commercial software development tools that leverage the Mono open source project in order to allow you to develop applications for Android, iOS, and OS X using C# and the .NET framework. The product that is used to develop Android apps is Xamarin.Android.

Why Xamarin.Android?

Before we take a dive into the architecture of Xamarin.Android, let's first discuss the question of why Xamarin.Android is our choice. Like any significant platform decision, one size does not fit all, and there are a number of things that should be considered. The following two lists identify some of the key benefits and drawbacks of using Xamarin.Android.

Benefits of using Xamarin.Android:

- Leverages existing C# and .NET skills

  Developers invest a great deal of time and energy in mastering the many features of the C# language and the effective use of the .NET framework. Yes, Java and all OO languages have many similarities, but there is a real cost associated with going from being proficient in C# and .NET to making the same claim in Java. Individuals and groups that have made a significant investment in C# and .NET and have a need to develop Android apps would be well served to at least consider Xamarin.Android.

- Reuse in cross-platform development

  While Xamarin.Android will not allow you to build a single app that can be deployed to Android, iOS, and WP8, it does give you the capability to reuse large portions of your code base across all of these platforms. In general, the user interface code and the code that deals with the device capabilities tend to be written for each platform, while things such as service client logic, client side validation, data caching, and client side data storage can potentially be reused, saving a significant amount of time.

Drawbacks of using Xamarin.Android:

- Licensing requirement

  Xamarin.Android as well as Xamarin.iOS and Xamarin.OS X are all commercial tools and must be licensed, so there is a tangible cost of entry. Check the Xamarin's website for current pricing.

- Waiting for updates

  There is some lag time between a new release of the Android platform and the corresponding release of Xamarin.Android.

- Performance and memory management

  In some cases, Xamarin.Android allocates both Java and C# objects to achieve some of the "magic" of developing in C#/.NET on an Android device. This has an impact on both the memory footprint and execution performance. Unfortunately, at this time, I do not have any objective data to quantify this impact. What I can report is that with two apps built and another one underway, my Android customers have not reported any concerns in this area.

- Distribution size

  There are a number of runtime libraries that must be distributed with a Xamarin.Android application. We will discuss the actual size and strategies for minimizing the distribution size in the last chapter.

While the list of drawbacks may seem extensive, in most cases, the impact of each can be minimized. If you are a group or individual that places a high value on the benefits, you should seriously consider Xamarin.Android.

What is Mono?

Mono is an open source, cross-platform implementation of a C# complier, and a **Common Language Runtime (CLR)** that is binary compatible with Microsoft .NET. The Mono CLR has been ported to many platforms, including Android, most Linux distributions, BSD, OS X, Windows, Solaris, and even some game consoles such as Wii and Xbox 360. In addition, Mono provides a static compiler that allows apps to be compiled for environments such as iOS and PS3.

Mono and Dalvik side by side

As you can recall from *Chapter 1, The Anatomy of an Android App*, Android apps run within the Dalvik VM, and we now know that Mono apps run within the Mono CLR. So how does a Xamarin.Android app run? A simple answer is that it uses both the Mono CLR and the Dalvik VM. The following diagram depicts how the runtimes co-exist:

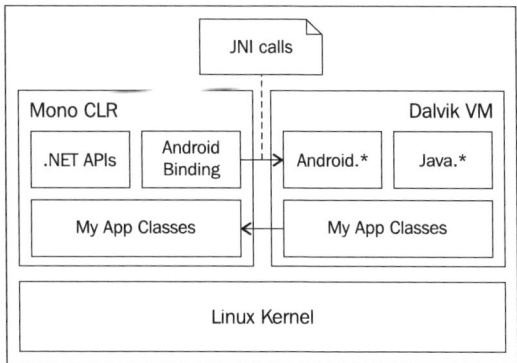

So, how do the Mono CLR and Dalvik VM work together in a Xamarin.Android app? The magic is accomplished through a concept called **peer objects** and a framework called the **Java Native Interface (JNI)**.

The Java Native Interface

Java Native Interface (JNI) is a framework that allows a non-Java code (such as C++ or C#) to call or be called by a Java code running inside a JVM. As you can see from the preceding diagram, JNI is a critical component in the overall Xamarin.Android architecture.

Peer objects

Peer objects are a pair of objects consisting of a managed object residing in the Mono CLR and a Java object residing in the Dalvik VM, which work together to perform the functions of a Xamarin.Android app.

Xamarin.Android is delivered with a set of assemblies called the Android binding libraries. Classes in the Android binding libraries correspond to the Java classes in the Android application framework, and the methods on the binding classes act as wrappers to call corresponding methods on Java classes. Binding classes are referred to as **Managed Callable Wrappers (MCW)**. Anytime you create a C# class that inherits from one of these binding classes, a corresponding Java proxy class is generated at build time. The Java proxy contains a generated override for each overridden method in your C# class and acts as a wrapper to call the corresponding method on the C# class.

The creation of peer objects can be initiated from within the Dalvik VM by the Android application framework or from within the Mono CLR by the code you write in the overridden methods. A reference between the two peer objects is kept by each instance of a MCW and can be accessed through the `Android.Runtime.IJavaObject.Handle` property.

The following diagram depicts how peer objects collaborate:

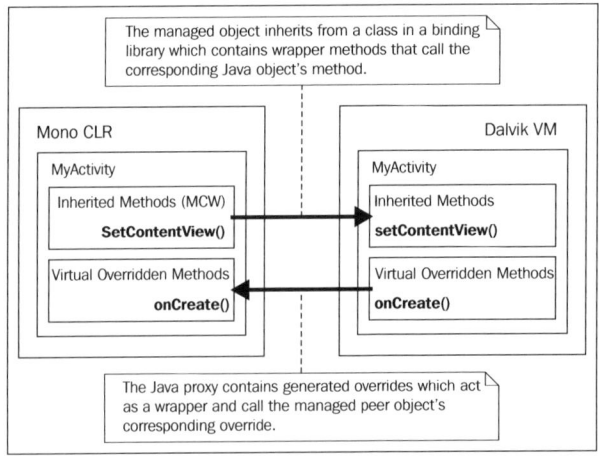

Xamarin.Android application packaging

In *Chapter 1*, *The Anatomy of an Android App*, we discussed Android packages (.apk files). Xamarin.Android creates the .apk files but also includes the following additional types of files:

- The C# code is stored as assemblies in the assembly folder of the archive
- The Mono runtime is packaged as native libraries

The Android bindings design

Core parts of Xamarin.Android are the bindings for the Android APIs. The Xamarin team focused a great deal in developing a consistent approach to creating the bindings so that a C# .NET developer would feel at home when using them. This has resulted in a number of key benefits as follows:

- The Android API feels natural to a C# .NET developer and allows the developer to explore the API using code completion and pop-up documentation from within the IDE
- C# developers can leverage the vast array of Java/Android examples and documentation that can be easily transformed for use with C# and Xamarin.Android

Design principles

A complete set of design principles can be found on the Xamarin website; we have included only a few for discussion:

- Allowing developers to subclass Java classes from the Android application framework
- Exposing a strongly typed API
- Exposing JavaBean properties as C# properties
- Exposing Java event listeners as C# delegates

C# properties

The JavaBean properties, the getter and setter methods, are transformed to C# properties, when appropriate. The following rules are used to determine when properties should be created:

- Read/write properties are created for the getter and setter method pairs

- Read-only properties are created for getters without corresponding setter methods

- No write-only properties are created for the rare case that only a setter exists

- Properties are not created when the type would be an array

 As you may be aware, Java does not have a property construct but instead follows a design pattern defined in the JavaBean specification. In order to define a property, a developer simply creates the public getter and setter methods with read-only properties that only provide a getter method.

Delegates

The Android APIs follow the Java pattern for defining and hooking up event listeners. The C# developers are more familiar with using delegates and events, so the Android bindings attempt to facilitate this using the following rules:

- When a `listener` callback has a void return, an event is generated based on the `EventHandler` delegate

- When a `listener` callback does not have a void return, a specific delegate is generated that supports the appropriate signature

These events or properties are only created under the following conditions:

- The Android event handling method has a prefix, for example, `setOnClickListener`

- The Android event handler has a void return type

- The Android event handler has a single parameter

Constants to enumerations

It is common in the Android APIs to see methods that accept or return an `int` type that must be mapped to a constant to determine its meaning. When possible, the Xamarin team creates a .NET enumeration to replace the constants and adjusts the appropriate methods to work with the enumerations. This provides a significant productivity gain by being able to use IntelliSense from within the IDE as well as enhancing the type safety of the methods.

Development environments

Developers have two choices when it comes to IDEs, Xamarin Studio or Visual Studio.

Xamarin Studio

Xamarin Studio is a customized version of the MonoDevelop IDE, which can be used to develop Android, iOS, and OS X applications. Xamarin Studio is available on both OS X and Windows and has many advanced features as follows:

- Code completion
- Smart syntax highlighting
- Code navigation
- Code tooltips
- Integrated debugging for mobile apps running in emulators or on devices
- Source control integration with Git and subversion built-in

The following screenshot shows Xamarin Studio with the Android user interface designer opened:

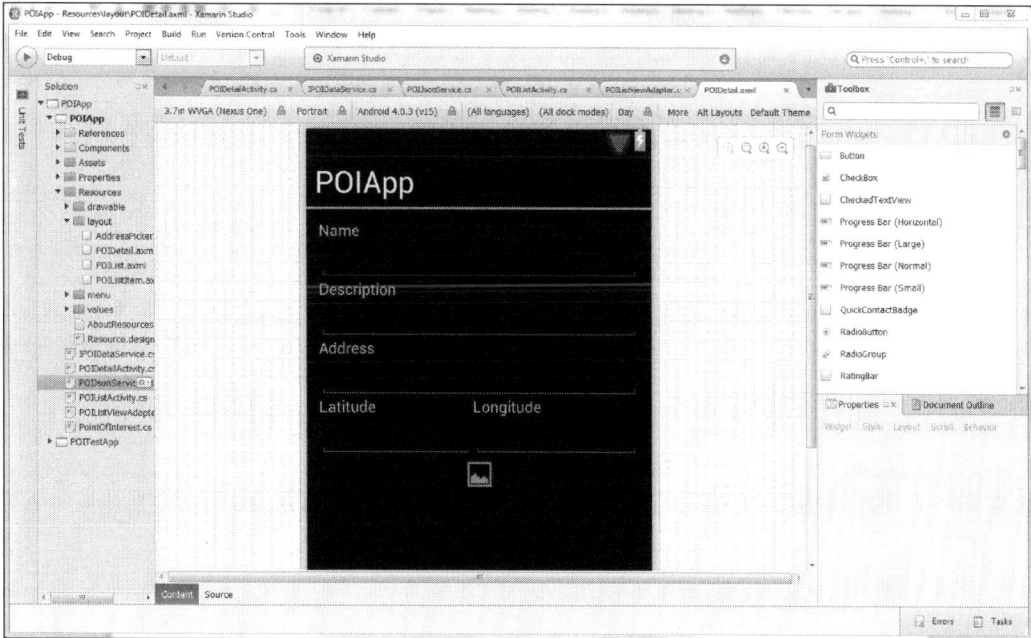

Xamarin for Visual Studio

Xamarin for Visual Studio is an add-in that supports the development of the Xamarin.Android apps. If you already have a license to Visual Studio and are comfortable with the environment, the add-in will likely be more appealing than Xamarin Studio because of the simplicity of adoption. The following screenshot shows Visual Studio 2012 with the Android user interface designer opened:

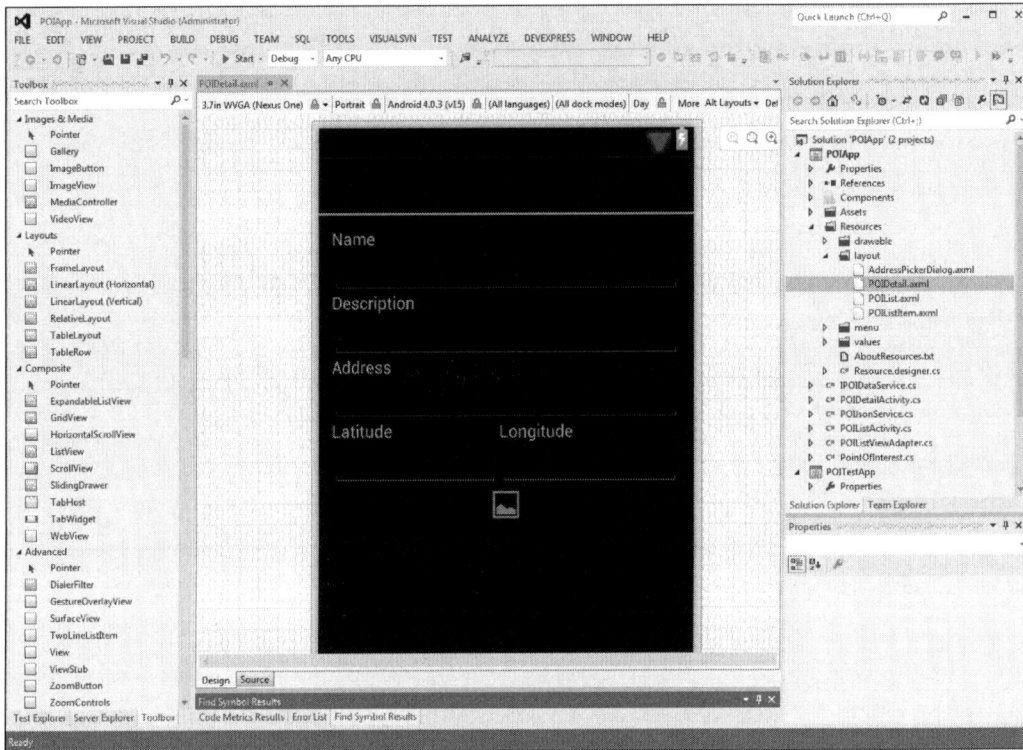

IDE comparison

The following table summarizes some of the pros and cons of adopting each IDE:

IDE	Pros	Cons
Xamarin Studio	It comes with Xamarin.Android	It does not support the use of TFS for source control
	No additional license is required	
	Runs on Windows and OS X	
Visual Studio	Most of the C# developers are already familiar and comfortable with Visual Studio	It requires an addition license
		It runs on Windows only
	It allows the use of TFS for source control, which is used in many .NET shops	

Compatibility

The solution and project files created and updated by Xamarin Studio are compatible with Visual Studio, making it easy to switch between the two environments throughout the duration of a project. This also allows the team members to adopt the tool that they are most comfortable with or that runs on their platform of choice.

Summary

In this chapter, we have discussed the architecture of Xamarin.Android and the magic of how it facilitates the creation of Android apps using C# and .NET. We also reviewed a set of benefits and drawbacks of adopting Xamarin.Android. In the next chapter, we will install Xamain.Android and create a project that we will build on for the remainder of the book.

3
Creating the Points of Interest App

In this chapter, we will move to the practical side of creating an app and cover the facilities Xamarin.Android provides developers for creating, executing, and debugging applications. This chapter covers the following topics:

- Overview of the sample app
- Installing Xamarin.Android
- Creating the sample app
- Running and debugging apps

The sample app

In this chapter, we will begin building a sample app that will be completed through the remaining chapters of the book. The app we have defined allows for the capture and management of points of interest and supports the following features:

- Capture information about points of interest, including name, description, address, latitude, longitude, and photos
- Save points of interest to a local file or files on the device using a combination of JSON text and image files
- List points of interest
- Capture address, latitude, and longitude of a point of interest using the devices location capabilities
- Capture and save a photo of a point of interest using the devices camera

Installing Xamarin.Android

Before we move on, we need to get Xamarin.Android installed. This section walks through installing Xamain.Android Version 4.8.3 on the Windows operating system. You may choose to install Xamarin.Android and work through the sample on Mac OSX, in which case you will encounter only minor deviations in some of the directions.

To install Xamarin.Android, perform the following steps:

1. Go to Xamarin.com, download the Windows installer, and launch it.

2. Click through the first two welcome pages and the agreement page until you come to the **Product selection** page. The installer allows the installation of both Xamarin.Android and Xamarin.iOS, as shown in the following screenshot. Xamarin.iOS will not be needed for the exercises in this book.

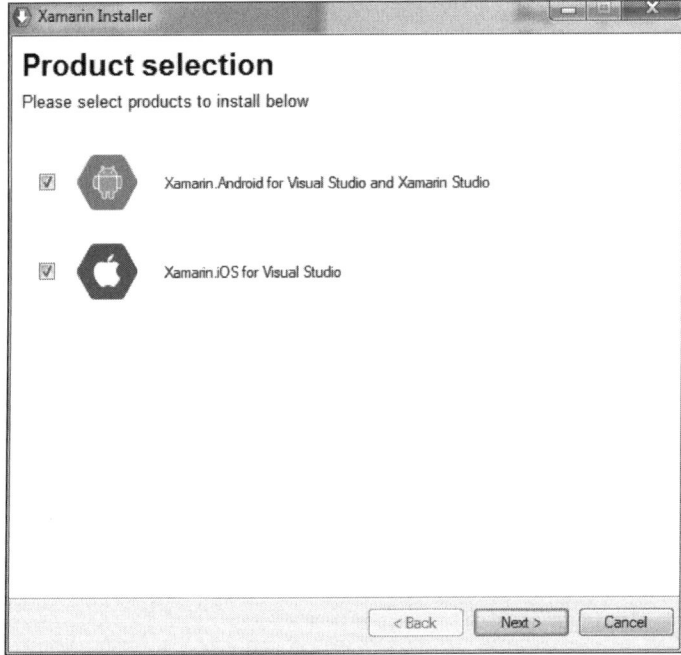

3. Uncheck **Xamarin.iOS for Visual Studio** and click on **Next**.

4. You should now be viewing the **Android SDK installation** page with the default installation location being displayed. There should be no need to make any changes on this page unless there is some form of conflict with a previously installed version of the Android SDK; click on **Next**, as shown in the following screenshot:

5. The **Requirements** page should be presented listing the various packages that will need to be installed along with the corresponding versions. Click on **Next** and click through the agreement pages presented.

6. An installation progress page will be displayed depicting the progress. As each component is installed, a check mark will be placed next to the component and once all items are installed, a final installation completion page will be displayed.

Creating the app

We are now ready to create the **Point of Interest** app as follows:

1. Launch Xamarin Studio.

2. From the **File** menu, navigate to **New | Solution**. The **New Solution** view will be presented as shown in the following screenshot:

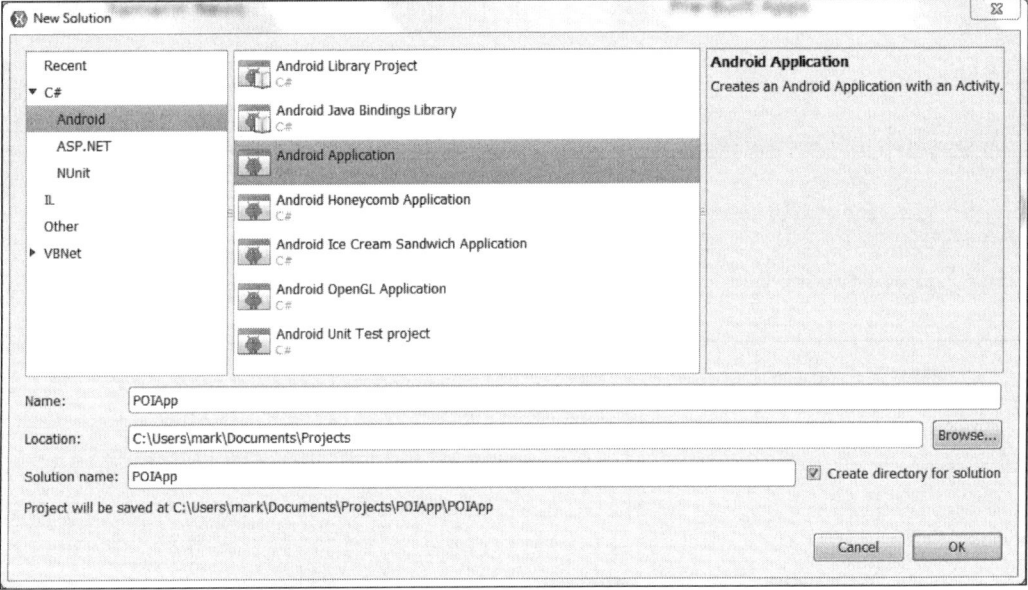

3. Select the **Android** section under C# on the left-hand side of the screen, Android Application from the middle list, and enter POIApp in the **Name** field. Review the project location and adjust if desired. Click on **OK**.

4. Xamarin Studio will create both a `solution` and `project` folder. The `project` folder will contain a default `MainActivity.cs` class and a `Main.axml` layout file.

Xamarin Studio IDE

After creating **POIApp**, the project will be opened within the environment. The following screenshot depicts Xamarin Studio after the project has been created:

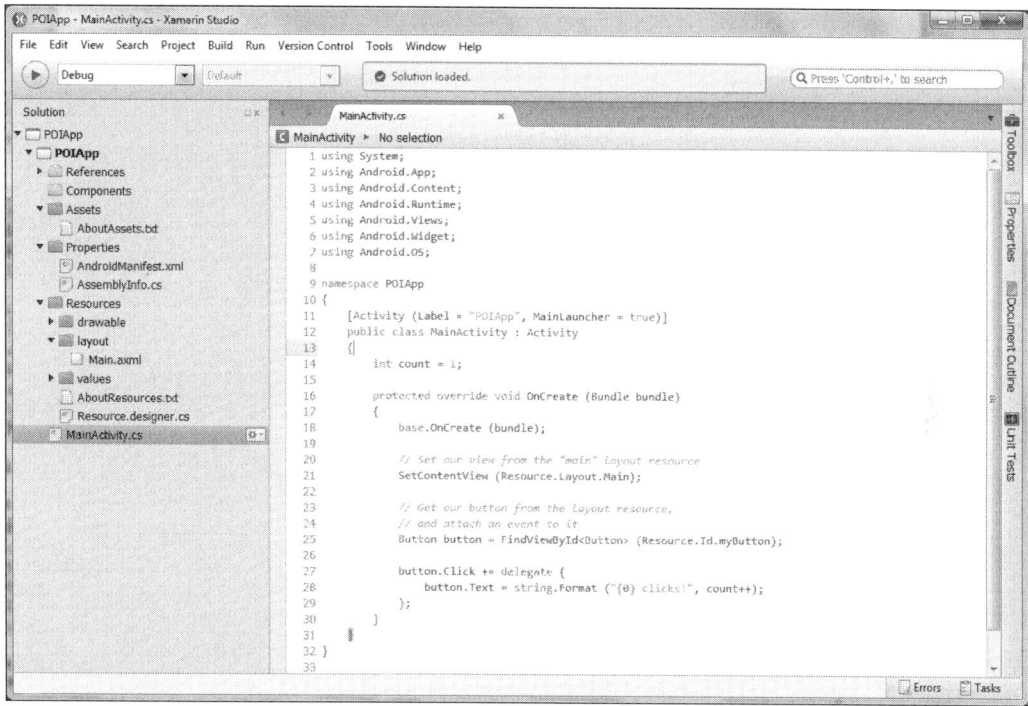

Xamarin Studio is organized like many modern IDEs with a set of menus at the top of the screen, a context-sensitive toolbar below it, and a series of dockable pads for viewing and manipulating various types of content. By default Xamarin Studio is configured with the following options:

- The **Solution** pad is docked on the left-hand side and allows you to explore the structure and content contained in the project

- Editor windows are in the middle and present the content of files for viewing and manipulation

- Task-specific pads are collapsed on the right-hand side and bottom, and can be expanded by hovering over the icon and caption

Additional pads can be accessed from **View** | **Pads**.

The Project Options View

There are numerous options that can be set, which affect the way an app is built and executed. These options can be adjusted from within the **Project Options** view.

Setting the target framework

The target framework setting determines which API level will be available to you during development and testing. If you review the Android platform version table from *Chapter 1, The Anatomy of an Android App*, you will find that Version 4.0.3 was released on December 16, 2011, and has the corresponding API level 15. Selecting this level for the target framework will allow the app to run on numerous older devices. If you want to experiment with a later API level, you can adjust the target framework setting.

In order to set the target framework, perform the following steps:

1. Select the POIApp project under the **POIApp** solution in the **Solution** pad.

2. Right-click on it and click on **Options**.

3. Select **Build | General** on the left-hand side.

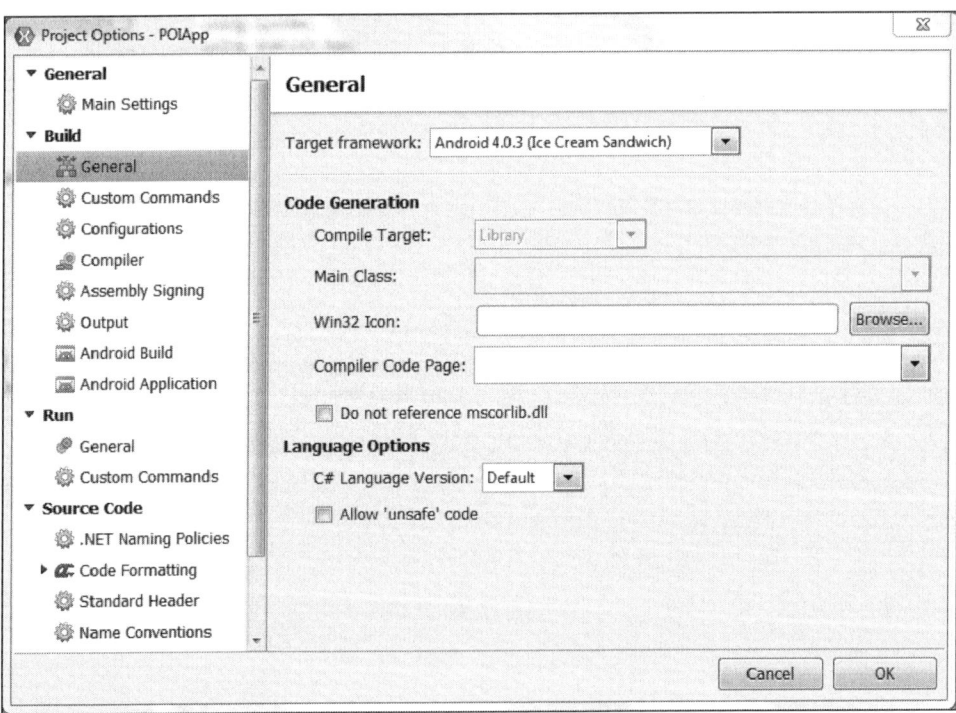

4. For the **Target framework** field, select **Android 4.0.3 (Ice Cream Sandwich)**.

5. Click on **OK**.

Setting the app icon and package name

Xamarin.Android provides a default icon and package name for apps. The icon will be displayed on the home view in Android as well as on the action bar at the top of each view.

In order to adjust the defaults for these settings, perform the following steps:

1. Using Windows Explorer, copy the image file ic_app.png from drawable present in the assets location to POIApp\ POIApp\Resources\drawable in the code bundle.

2. From within Xamarin Studio, navigate to Resources\drawable, right-click on it, and click on **Add Files**.

3. Navigate to POIApp\Resources\drawable in the code bundle, select ic_app.png, and click on **Open**. You should now see ic_app.png listed under drawable in the **Solution** pad, making it available for use within the app.

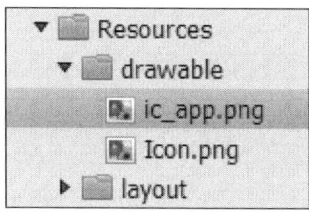

4. Select the POIApp project, right-click on it, and click on **Options**

5. Select **Build | Android Application**.

6. Change the **Package** name to POIApp. This will cause the resulting APK file to be named as POIApp.apk.

7. Change **Application icon** selection to @drawable/ic_app.

8. Click on **OK**.

We will cover additional options in *Chapter 9, Deploying Your App*, as we prepare the app for deployment.

The initial activity

When an app is selected from the home screen on an Android device, the Android OS creates an instance of the activity in the application you have declared to be the launch activity. When developing with the Android SDK, this is specified in the `AndroidManifest.xml` file. The following code excerpt from `AndroidManifest.xml` shows how to specify that `MainActivity` should be launched first:

```xml
<activity android:label="POIApp"
  android:name="poiapp.MainActivity">
<intent-filter>
<action android:name="android.intent.action.MAIN" />
<category android:name="android.intent.category.LAUNCHER" />
</intent-filter>
</activity>
```

Xamarin.Android provides a more convenient method of specifying this by the use of .NET attributes. These .NET attributes are used at build time to construct the `ApplicationManifest.xml` file so that you rarely ever need to worry about working with the file directly. In the case of specifying the initial activity to launch, setting `MainLauncher` to `true` does the job, as seen in the following code example:

```csharp
[Activity (Label = "POIApp", MainLauncher = true)]
public class MainActivity : Activity
{
   . . .
}
```

Running and debugging the app

The way in which you run and debug apps is very important to developers as it has a big impact on productivity and timelines. Xamarin Studio and the Android emulator team up to make the testing and debugging cycle as painless as possible. Let's go through the steps:

1. Start a debugging session by clicking on the **Start** button on the left-hand side of the taskbar, by pressing *F5*, or by navigating to **Run** | **Start Debugging**.

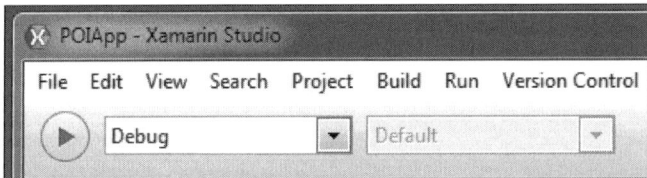

2. Select **MonoForAnroid_API_15 (emulator)** from the list and click on **Start Emulator**. You will need to wait for the emulator to start up.

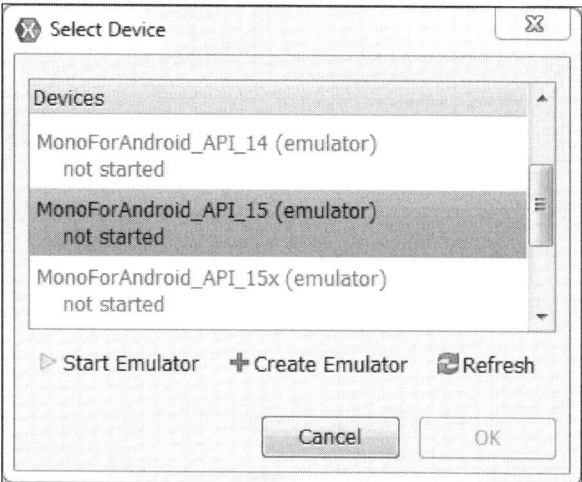

3. Select **MonoForAnroid_API_15 (emulator-5554)** at the top of the **Devices** list and click on **OK**. Xamarin Studio will deploy the compiled app to the emulator. The progress of the deployment can be monitored from the status view in the middle of the toolbar and from the **Application Output** pad at the bottom of the IDE.

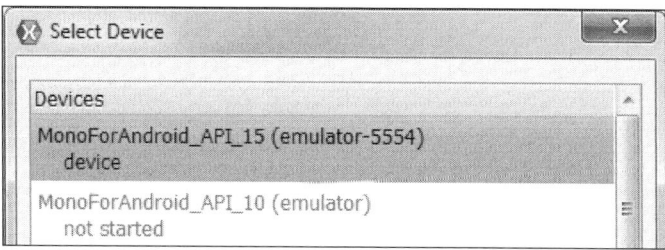

4. Toggle to the Android emulator and unlock the screen. The POI app will be present.

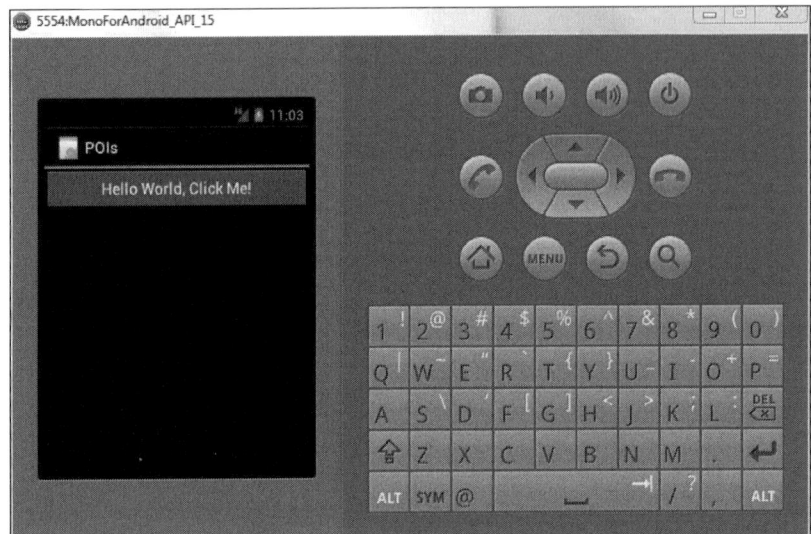

 The Android emulator is used for testing Android apps during the development process. The left-hand side of the screen depicts what would be seen on a device and the right-hand side provides keys that replicate the device hardware.

5. Click on the **Hello World** button and the app will increment a counter and update the button's caption.

6. Toggle back to Xamarin Studio and stop the app by clicking on the **Stop** button at the extreme left of the toolbar.

7. Open `MainActivity.cs` and set a breakpoint on line 21 by clicking on the left margin of the editor, just to the left of the line number.

8. Restart the app by clicking on the **Start** button. Since the Android emulator is still running, you will not need to make a device selection. The app will stop at the breakpoint previously set.

```
19
20                // Set our view from the "main" layout resource
21        SetContentView (Resource.Layout.Main);
22
```

9. You will notice a set of debug controls present in the toolbar. There are controls to continue execution, namely step over current line, step into current function, and step out of current function.

10. You will also notice a new set of pads related to the debugging apps present at the bottom of the IDE. These pads allow for viewing of objects, breakpoints, threads, and the call stack.

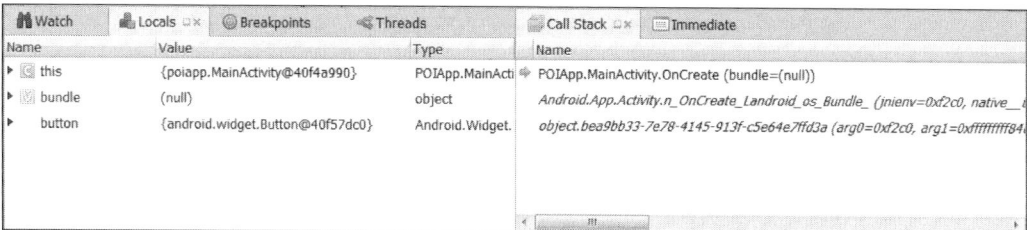

11. Click on **Step Over** twice to watch the progress of the execution, and then click on **Continue** to let the app start.

As you can see from this section, Xamarin Studio and the Android emulator facilitates a robust intuitive way of executing and debugging applications.

Creating and customizing emulators

The emulators presented when we ran our app were set up as part of the Xamarin install. You can customize these existing emulators or create your own in order to adjust the features and software configuration for the device being emulated.

In order to modify an existing emulator, perform the following steps:

1. From the main menu bar, select **Tools | Open Android Emulator Manager**.

2. In the **Android Virtual Device Manager** dialog box, select the AVD named **MonoForAndroid_API15** and click on **Edit**.

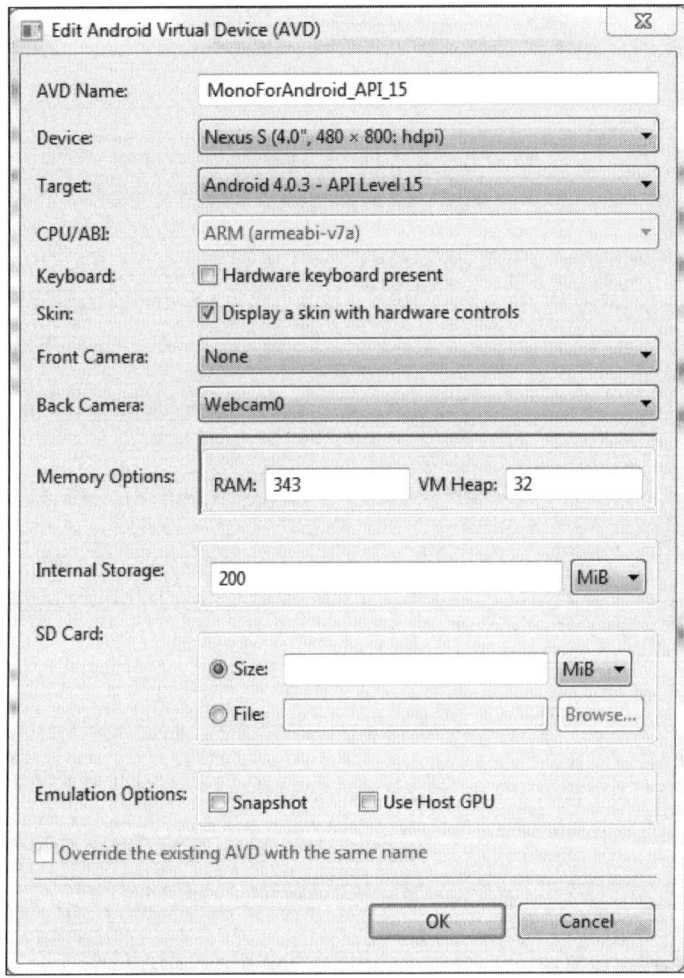

3. Note the **Target** setting; this specifies the version of the Android platform and the API level that will be used for the emulator.

4. Set the **Device** field to **Nexus S**, reset the **Target** field to **Android 4.0.3**, if needed, uncheck the **Hardware keyboard present** option, and click on **OK**.

5. Run POIApp using the modified configuration.

There are many options that can be modified in order to emulate any device and configuration needed. The **Android Virtual Device Manager** dialog box also has a tab named **Device Definitions** that can be used to set up the devices that are available when configuring an AVD. The following screenshot shows what can be configured as part of the device definition:

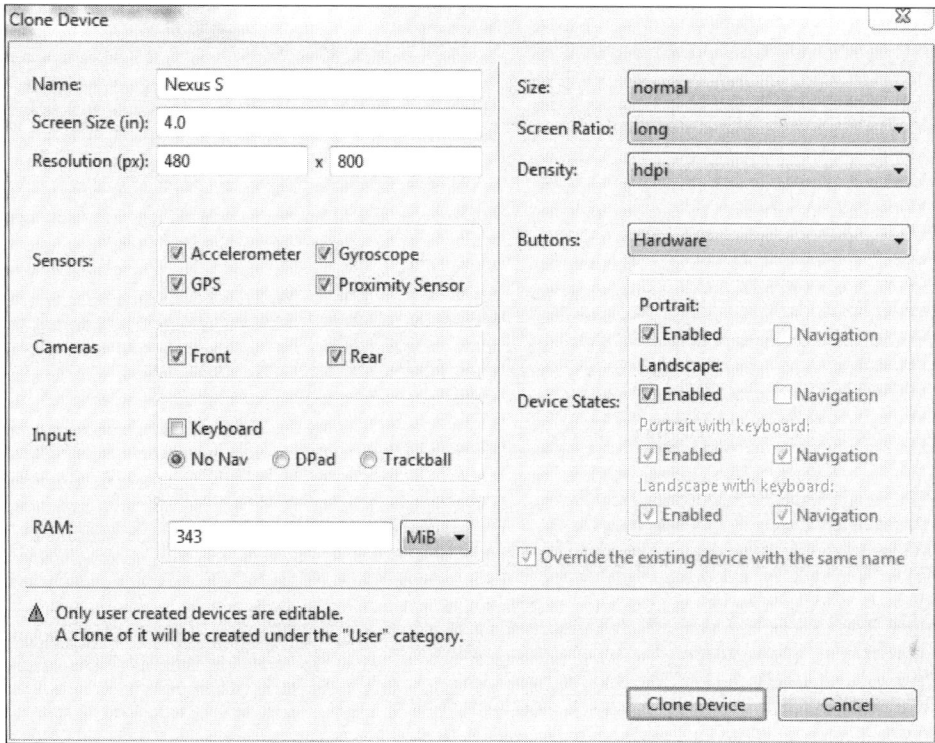

Using the x86 emulator

Android provides an x86 emulator that can speed up development considerably due to faster start and execution times for the AVD. The x86 emulator is not a part of the base Xamarin install, but the directions for installation can be found on the Xamarin website as well as the Android developer website. A very specific version may be required, particularly if using OSX Mavericks, so we will not replicate the directions here.

Once installed, you can take advantage of the x86 emulator by the selected Intel Atom (x86) for the CPU/ABI when editing an AVD configuration.

Debugging with an Android device

Apps can be executed and debugged on actual devices with the same simplicity of working with an emulator. To prepare for using a physical device, you need to perform a few steps as follows:

1. Enable USB debugging on the device.
2. Install an appropriate USB driver for the device (Windows only).

Enabling USB debugging

In order to enable USB debugging on a device with Android 4.0 and newer, perform the following steps:

1. For devices running Android 4.2 or newer, there is an extra step; **Developer options** is initially hidden. Navigate to **Settings | About phone** and tap **Build number** seven times. On some configurations, the exact menu structure may differ. On my HTC One with Android 4.3, the menu is **Settings | About | Software information | More**.
2. Navigate to **Settings | Developer options**.
3. Click on **USB debugging**.

Installing a USB driver

Windows users are required to install a USB driver that matches their device; please refer to the Android developer website under a section titled **Using Hardware Devices** for more details or consult your device manufacturer.

OS X users should be good to go.

Running apps on a device

After completing the previous steps, simply connect the device to your development computer with a USB cable, start the app from Xamarin Studio, and choose the actual hardware device from the device selection view rather than starting an emulator.

Behind the scenes

It is interesting at this point to take a quick look at a few of the things that go on behind the scenes, which we previously discussed.

Peer object

Let's start with the peer object (proxy object) discussed in *Chapter 2, Xamarin.Android Architecture.* Navigate to `POIApp\POIApp\obj\Debug\android\src\poiapp` in the code bundle in Windows XP and open `MainActivity.java` using Notepad. The following code listing depicts some of the key pieces of the source file:

```
package poiapp;

public class MainActivity extends android.app.Activity implements
  mono.android.IGCUserPeer
{
  . . .

  public void onCreate (android.os.Bundle p0)
  {
    n_onCreate (p0);
  }

  private native void n_onCreate (android.os.Bundle p0);
  . . .

}
```

Note the following points:

- The `MainActivity` class extends `android.app.Activity`, which is what you would expect
- An `onCreate()` proxy method is created that calls the native method `n_onCreate()`, which points to the overridden `OnCreate()` method in our managed C# class
- The `MainActivity` class has a static initializing block and a constructor that establishes the link between the Java class and it's managed C# peer, including initializing `n_onCreate()`

The AndroidManifest.xml file

Navigate to `POIApp\POIApp\obj\Debug\android` in the code bundle and open the `AndroidManifest.xml` file. The following code listing depicts a portion of the manifest file:

```xml
<?xml version="1.0" encoding="utf-8"?>
<manifest
  xmlns:android="http://schemas.android.com/apk/res/android"
    android:versionCode="1" android:versionName="1.0"
      package="POIApp.POIApp">
  <uses-sdk android:minSdkVersion="15" />
  <application android:label="POIApp"
    android:name="mono.android.app.Application"
      android:debuggable="true">
    <activity android:label="POIs"
      android:name="poiapp.MainActivity">
      <intent-filter>
        <action android:name="android.intent.action.MAIN" />
        <category android:name="android.intent.category.LAUNCHER"
          />
      </intent-filter>
    </activity>
    . . .
  </application>
  <uses-permission android:name="android.permission.INTERNET" />
</manifest>
```

Note the following points:

- The target SDK is set to 15 in the `<uses-sdk\>` element
- The initial activity is set using the `<category\>` element within the activity definition

Summary

In this chapter we have started a sample app that we will complete through the remaining chapters of the book, and we have demonstrated the facilities we have for executing and debugging apps. In the next chapter we will continue with building of the app by building a set of data-persistence capabilities.

4
Creating a Data Storage Mechanism

We now turn our attention to data storage requirements; we need a way to store and retrieve **Point of Interest (POI)** data. This chapter covers the following topics:

- Approaches to data storage solutions
- Creating the POI entity class
- Creating the POI data storage interface
- Implementing the POI data storage service
- Using Xamarin.Android unit tests to support development

Data storage solutions fall into two general categories, web services and local storage. While many real-world mobile apps rely on web services, we will focus on a local storage solution for a couple of reasons. First, it eliminates the need to maintain a hosted service for the example to work, and second, we simply do not have sufficient time to adequately deal with creating and accessing a web service solution in this book.

There are a number of solutions that can be used for storing data locally. **SQLite** is a lightweight transactional database engine that is delivered with the Android platform. SQLite is widely used on mobile platforms such as Android and iOS as well as on embedded systems of all types. SQLite is a great solution if you need the robust capabilities that a relational engine provides, but we have much simpler requirements; a simple file-based solution will be adequate for POIApp.

As such, we have decided to go with a solution that stores the POI data as local files. This leads us to our next decision: how do we structure the data inside the file? JSON and XML are the two predominant standards that are used to store structured data in a text format. XML tends to be more verbose and is used in conjunction with SOAP/WSDL based web services. Data encoded with JSON is smaller than the equivalent XML, and thus, JSON has gained a lot of traction in the RESTful web-service community. Either of these standards meet our needs. The example presented in this chapter uses a JSON-based solution. In order to accommodate other implementations in the future we will, however, establish a standard interface for the storage service. This means that other implementations such as a web-service version of the XML-based version could be developed and plugged in with a minimal effort.

Creating the Point of Interest entity class

The first class that is needed is the one that represents the primary focus of the application, a Point of Interest class. POIApp will allow the following attributes to be captured for a Point of Interest:

- Id
- Name
- Description
- Address
- Latitude
- Longitude

The POI entity class can be nothing more than a simple .NET class, which houses these attributes.

To create a POI entity class, perform the following steps:

1. Select the POIApp project from the **Solution** pad in Xamarin Studio. Select the POIApp project and not the solution which is the top-level node in the **Solution** pad.
2. Right-click on it and select **New File**.

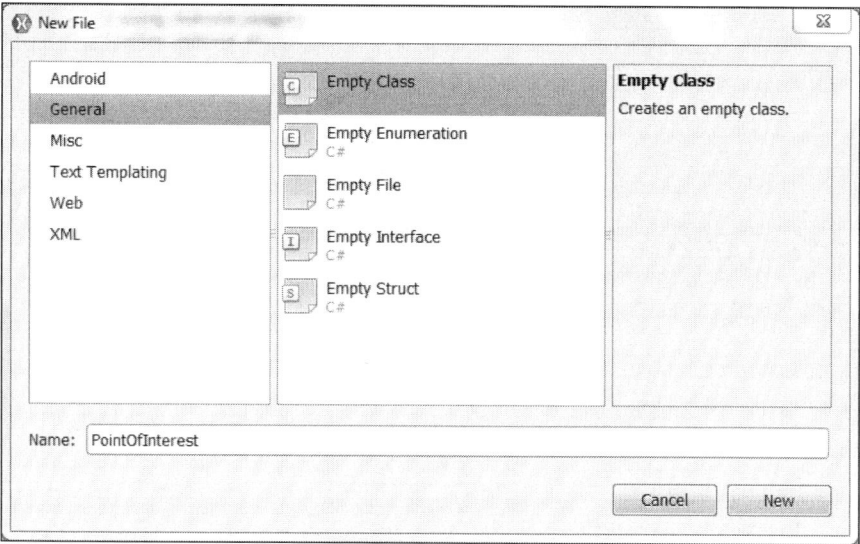

3.   On the left-hand side of the **New File** dialog box, select **General**.

4.   At the top of the template list, in the middle of the dialog box, select **Empty Class (C#)**.

5.   Enter the name `PointOfInterest` and click on **OK**. The class will be created in the `POIApp` project folder.

6.   Change the visibility of the class to public and fill in the attributes based on the list previously identified.

The following code snippet is from `9169_04_Codes\POIApp\POIApp\PointOfInterest.cs` from the code bundle available for this book:

```
public class PointOfInterest
{
  public int? Id { get; set;}
  public string Name { get; set; }
  public string Description { get; set; }
  public string Address { get; set; }
  public double? Latitude { get; set; }
  public double? Longitude { get; set; }
}
```

Note that the `Id`, `Latitude`, and `Longitude` attributes are all marked as nullable. In the case of `Latitude` and `Longitude`, (0,0) is actually a valid location so a null value indicates the attributes have never been set. The `Id` attribute is required but having a null value tells `POIJsonService` to assign an actual value when the POI is saved.

Creating the POI storage interface

Now, we need to create a standard interface that will define the methods provided by the storage service. The interface will need to allow basic CRUD (create, read, update, and delete) operations. We would also like to provide basic caching capabilities. Caching can dramatically enhance app responsiveness by storing data that will likely be accessed multiple times in the memory locally and preventing multiple reads from a file or accesses to a web service.

To create the data service interface, perform the following steps:

1. Select the `POIApp` project in the **Solution** pad in Xamarin Studio.
2. Right-click on it and select **New File**.
3. On the left-hand side of the **New File** dialog, select **General**.
4. At the top of the template list, in the middle of the dialog, select **Empty Interface (C#)**.
5. Enter the name `IPOIDataService` and click on **OK**.
6. Fill in the methods to support the CRUD operations and caching. You will need to also add a collection property for the caching of POIs based on `IReadOnlyList`. The use of `IReadOnlyList` ensures that POIs cannot be added directly to the cache but must be added or deleted through the CRUD operations.

The following example shows the interface's definition from the `9169_04_Codes\POIApp\POIApp\IPOIDataService.cs` from the code bundle of this book. Note that in this example, `SavePOI()` accounts for the create and update portion of CRUD.

```
public interface IPOIDataService
{
  IReadOnlyList<PointOfInterest> POIs { get; }
  void RefreshCache();
  PointOfInterest GetPOI (int id);
  void SavePOI(PointOfInterest poi);
  void DeletePOI(PointOfInterest poi);
}
```

Implementing the POI storage services

Now that we know what the POI service needs to do, let's create an actual implementation:

1. Create a class called POIJsonService.

2. Change the visibility of the class to public, and specify that POIJsonService implements the IPOIDataService interface.

3. Place the cursor over IPOIDataService, right-click on it, and go to **Refactor | Implement interface**. Use the arrow keys to move the prompt to the location in the file where you would like to place the implementation methods and press *Enter*.

You should now have a class with method stubs for all the required methods for the IPOIDataService interface. The following example shows what the class should contain at this point:

```
public class POIJsonService : IPOIDataService
{
  public POIJsonService ()
  {
  }

  #region IPOIDataService implementation

  public void RefreshCache ()
  {
    throw new NotImplementedException ();
  }

  public PointOfInterest GetPOI (int id)
  {
    throw new NotImplementedException ();
  }

  public void SavePOI (PointOfInterest poi)
  {
    throw new NotImplementedException ();
  }

  public void DeletePOI (PointOfInterest poi)
```

```
    {
      throw new NotImplementedException ();
    }

    public System.Collections.Generic.IReadOnlyList<PointOfInterest>
  POIs {
      get {
        throw new NotImplementedException ();
      }
    }

    #endregion
  }
```

The next step is to fill in the logic for each method and write any supporting methods that may be required.

Using Xamarin.Android NUnitLite

You may be familiar with a process called **test-driven development (TDD)**. At a high-level, the approach proposes that you create automated unit test cases to test the features that your software will need to support and use these test cases to drive the development and unit testing cycle.

This chapter will not cover the concepts behind test-driven development in detail, but we will introduce a feature delivered with Xamarin.Android, which supports teams using TDD. This feature is **NUnitLite**. NUnitLite is a lightweight, open source testing framework which is based on the same ideas as NUnit. NUnitLite has been designed to use minimal resources, making it ideal for embedded and mobile software development.

When working with NUnitLite, you create classes called test fixtures. These classes contain test methods that are used to test the various facets of the testing target, in our case, the POIJsonService class. To designate a class as a test fixture or a method as a test method, NUnitLite uses the .NET attributes. Once the test fixtures and test methods have been created, Xamarin.Android provides a user interface that allows the tests to be executed within the Android emulator or on a device.

To start using NUnitLite, we need to create a test project in the **Solution** that we have been working with.

To create a test project, perform the following steps:

1. Select the **POIApp** solution from the **Solution** pad in Xamarin Studio.

2. Right-click on it and select **Add New Project**.

3. On the left-hand side of the **New Project** dialog, go to **C#** | **Android**.

4. In the template list, in the middle of the dialog box, select the **Android Unit Test** project.

5. Enter POITestApp for the name and click on **OK**. The new unit test project is created and added to the **POIApp** solution.

6. Go to the **Options** dialog for the new project, and set the **Package name** to POITestApp and the **Target framework** to 4.0.3.

You will notice that the new unit test project has the following files:

- MainActivity.cs: This activity inherits from TestSuiteActivity and provides a test suite user interface when we run our tests. Basically, it allows us to run our tests and see the results.

- TestsSample.cs: This class acts as a test fixture and allows us to add test methods that will exercise the features provided by POIJsonService.

Now, we need to create the test methods in order to exercise the features of our data service. Initially, when we execute the tests, they will fail because the methods are only stubs and immediately throw an exception, NotImplementedException. As we fill in the actual logic for our data service, the tests will begin to pass.

Setting up for tests

NUnitLite provides a place to execute any initialization code that may be required by the tests. In our case, we need to create an instance of our data service, which the test methods will later interact with. The Setup() method is the perfect place since it will be called before each test.

1. Rename the TestsSample.cs file to POITestFixture.cs. Rename the corresponding class inside the file as well.

2. In **POITestApp**, select **References**, right-click on it, and select **Edit References**. Select the **Projects** tab in the **Edit References** dialog, check on the POIApp project, and click on **OK**. POITestApp needs to reference POIApp so that it can work with IPOIDataService and POIJsonService.

3. Open the POITestFixture class and within it declare a private variable of type IPOIDataService. In the Setup() method initialize the private variable to an instance of POIJsonService:

```
[TestFixture]
public class POITestFixture
```

```
{
    IPOIDataService _poiService;

    [SetUp]
    public void Setup ()
    {
        _poiService = new POIJsonService ();
    }
}
```

Creating the test methods

Now the real work begins; we need to create test methods to test each significant scenario. In the case of the data service, we need to be sure of covering the following:

- Creating a new POI
- Updating an existing POI
- Deleting an existing POI

There are many more scenarios we could choose to test, but the preceding small set should help to verify if the basics of our data service are functioning.

The Create POI test

The first test method we will start with is CreatePOI() and, as the name implies, we will test the process of creating and saving a new POI. To accomplish this, we need to perform the following steps:

1. Create a new instance of PointOfInterest and fill out some attributes.
2. Call SavePOI() on the data service.
3. Save the Id for the newly created POI.
4. Refresh the cache to ensure whether the new POI was appropriately saved and can be restored from storage.
5. Call GetPOI() to retrieve the POI, based on the saved ID.
6. Use the Assert class to ascertain that the POI was retrieved (the reference is not null) and the name of the POI is what you expected it to be.

The following code shows an implementation of CreatePOI():

```
[Test]
public void CreatePOI ()
```

```
{
    PointOfInterest newPOI = new PointOfInterest ();
    newPOI.Name = "New POI";
    newPOI.Description = "POI to test creating a new POI";
    newPOI.Address = "100 Main Street\nAnywhere, TX 75069";
    _poiService.SavePOI (newPOI);

    int testId = newPOI.Id.Value;

    // refresh the cache to be sure the data was
    // saved appropriately
    _poiService.RefreshCache ();

    // verify if the newly create POI exists
    PointOfInterest poi = _poiService.GetPOI (testId);
    Assert.NotNull (poi);
    Assert.AreEqual (poi.Name, "New POI");
}
```

The Update POI test

Next, we will implement UpdatePOI(); again, as the name implies, we want to test the updating and existing POIs. We should strive to make our tests independent of each other, which means that UpdatePOI should not rely on CreatePOI() to run successfully. As such, UpdatePOI will first create a new POI that will then be updated. UpdatePOI() will perform the following steps:

1. Create a new instance of PointOfInterest and fill out some attributes.
2. Call SavePOI() on the data service.
3. Save the Id for the newly created POI.
4. Refresh the cache to ensure that the new POI was appropriately saved and can be restored from storage.
5. Call GetPOI() to retrieve the POI, based on the saved ID.
6. Set the Description property to a new value.
7. Call SavePOI() to save the updates.
8. Refresh the cache to ensure that the updated POI was appropriately saved and can be restored from storage.
9. Call GetPOI() to retrieve the POI, based on the saved ID.
10. Use the Assert class to be sure that the POI was retrieved (the reference is not null) and the description of the POI is what you expected it to be.

The following code shows an implementation of `UpdatePOI()`:

```
[Test]
public void UpdatePOI ()
{
  PointOfInterest testPOI = new PointOfInterest ();
  testPOI.Name = "Update POI";
  testPOI.Description = "POI being saved so we can test update";
  testPOI.Address = "100 Main Street\nAnywhere, TX 75069";
  _poiService.SavePOI (testPOI);

  int testId = testPOI.Id.Value;

  // refresh the cache to be sure the data and
  // poi was saved appropriately
  _poiService.RefreshCache ();

  PointOfInterest poi = _poiService.GetPOI (testId);
  poi.Description = "Updated Description for Update POI";
  _poiService.SavePOI (poi);

  // refresh the cache to be sure the data was
  // updated appropriately
  _poiService.RefreshCache ();

  PointOfInterest poi = _poiService.GetPOI (testId);
  Assert.NotNull (poi);
  Assert.AreEqual (poi.Description, "Updated Description for
    Update POI");
}
```

The DeletePOI() test

Finally, we will implement `DeletePOI()`. Again, we want `DeletePOI()` to be independent of other tests, so we will first need to create a POI which will be deleted later. On calling `DeletePOI()`, the following steps will be performed:

1. Create a new instance of `PointOfInterest` and fill out some attributes.
2. Call `SavePOI()` on the data service.
3. Save the `Id` for the newly created POI.
4. Refresh the cache to ensure that the new POI was appropriately saved and can be restored from storage.

5. Call GetPOI() to retrieve the POI, based on the saved ID.

6. Call DeletePOI() to delete the POI file and remove it from the cache.

7. Refresh the cache to ensure that the updated POI was appropriately deleted.

8. Call GetPOI() to retrieve the POI, based on the saved ID.

Use the Assert class to ensure that the POI is not found (the reference is null). The following code show an implementation of DeletePOI():

```
[Test]
public void DeletePOI ()
{
  PointOfInterest testPOI = new PointOfInterest ();
  testPOI.Name = "Delete POI";
  testPOI.Description = "POI being saved so we can test delete";
  testPOI.Address = "100 Main Street\nAnywhere, TX 75069";
  _poiService.SavePOI (testPOI);

  int testId = testPOI.Id.Value;

  // refresh the cache to be sure the data and
  // poi was saved appropriately
  _poiService.RefreshCache ();

  PointOfInterest deletePOI = _poiService.GetPOI (testId);
  Assert.IsNotNull (deletePOI);
  _poiService.DeletePOI (deletePOI);

  // refresh the cache to be sure the data was
  // deleted appropriately
  _poiService.RefreshCache ();

  PointOfInterest poi = _poiService.GetPOI (testId);
  Assert.Null (poi);
}
```

Executing the tests

Now that the tests have been developed, we are ready to execute them. To do this, we simply run the test app using the Android emulator or a physical device.

To execute the tests in an emulator, perform the following steps:

1. Run **POITestApp** using the Android emulator. Note that the **POITestApp** is not set as the **Startup Project**, so you will need to select the project when you select run. You can make **POITestApp** as the **Startup Project** by selecting it, right-clicking on it, and choosing **Set** as **Startup Project**. Once **POITestApp** is running, you should see the following screen when the app has been deployed and started:

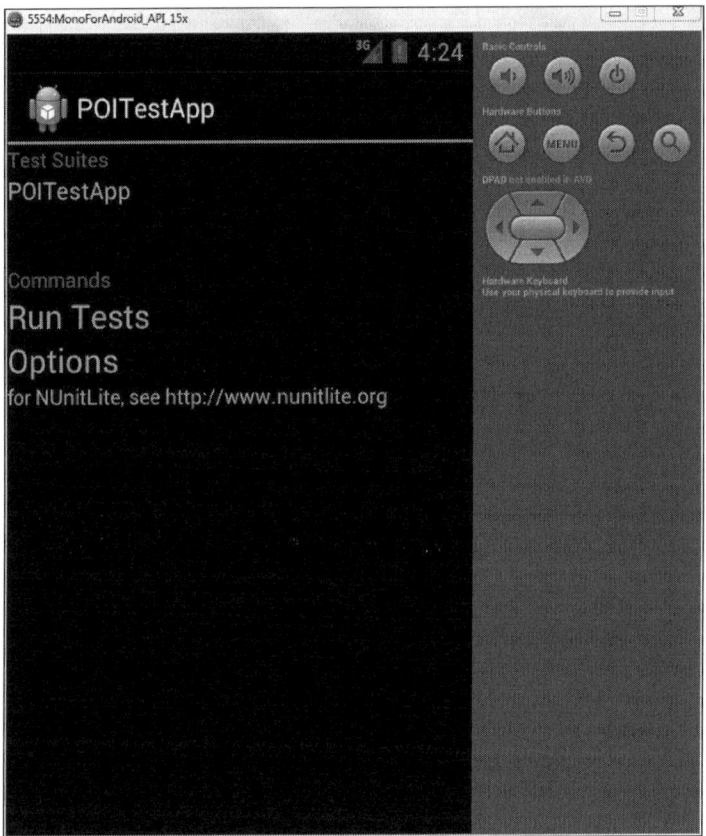

2. Execute the tests by clicking on the **Run Tests** label. You should see a red message label indicating that all the tests have failed. You can drill down into the tests to see the failure details. The tests currently fail because the stub methods throw exceptions, which is not the expected behavior.

So far, we have created a skeleton of `POIJsonService` and have a suite of automated tests to test the CRUD methods. It is now time to focus on filling in the logic so that all the tests pass.

Json.NET

One of the first decisions we need to make regarding the implementation of the services is how we will deal with JSON serialization, meaning how will we get our .NET objects converted to JSON for storage and vice versa. There are a number of options available, including `DataContractJsonSerailzier` from .NET. Json.NET is an open source library created by *James Newton-King*, and this is definitely worth considering:

- It's small and fast
- It's reliable
- It's available for many platforms including as a free component in the Xamarin Component Store
- It makes simple tasks extremely simple to accomplish

With these characteristics in mind, we will go with Json.NET for serialization.

Downloading Json.NET

To download and add Json.NET to the `POIApp` project, perform the following steps:

1. Select the components package in `POIApp`, right-click on it, and select **Get More Components**.

2. Enter `Json.NET` in the search field in the upper-left corner of the form, as shown in the following screenshot:

3. Select **Json.NET** to see the details page and select **Add to App**. The **Json.NET library** will be downloaded and added to your project.

Adding Json.NET to POITestApp is easy because we have already downloaded it; simply select the components package in a project, right-click on it, and select **Edit Components**, and then select **Add to Project**, which is next to **Json.NET**.

Implementing and testing the POIJsonService methods

We are now ready to start building the methods on POIJsonService and incrementally test them. We will store POIs as individual JSON text files in a single directory using a naming scheme that incorporates the ID (poi<id>.json). POIJsonService will need to know which directory to locate these JSON files in. To facilitate this, we will create a private string that will hold the storage location path, which will be passed to the constructor when the service is created. The constructor should check whether the directory exists and create it if it doesn't.

We would also like to build the cache so that it will be ready for use. We can accomplish this with a call to RefreshCache().

The following code is from the code bundle of this book:

```
private string _storagePath;

public POIJsonService (string storagePath)
{
  _storagePath = storagePath;

  // create the storage path if it does not exist
  if (!Directory.Exists(_storagePath))
    Directory.CreateDirectory(_storagePath);

  RefreshCache ();
}
```

Now that the constructor accepts a storage location, we need to go back and update the Setup method in POITestFixture.

During testing, we would want to store our files in the sandbox associated with our application. This location can be obtained from the Environment.GetFolderPath() method.

We should also delete any existing JSON files found in this folder prior to executing the test so that we know the starting state for the test.

The following code shows an updated Setup method:

```
[SetUp]
public void Setup ()
{
  string storagePath =
  Environment.GetFolderPath (Environment.SpecialFolder.MyDocuments);
```

```
_poiService = new POIJsonService (storagePath);

   // clear any existing json files
   foreach (string filename in Directory.EnumerateFiles(storagePath,
     "*.json")) {
     File.Delete (filename);
   }
}
```

Implementing caching

We will need a private collection to facilitate the caching of the POIs, and the `RefreshCache()` method will be used to load the POIs into the collection. Add the following `List` definition to the `POIJsonService` class. You will need to use the `System.Collections.Generic` namespace.

```
private List<PointOfInterest> _pois = new List<PointOfInterest>();
```

We need to expose this list as a read-only collection to fulfill the interface requirements of `IPOIDataService`. The following code shows what is needed:

```
public IReadOnlyList<PointOfInterest> POIs {
   get { return _pois; }
}
```

We now need to implement the `RefreshCache()` method to load the cache when `POIJsonService` is constructed. Once constructed, the service will maintain the cache each time `SavePOI()` or `DeletePOI()` is called. Let's look at how to create a .NET object from a JSON text file using Json.NET:

1. First, we read the entire contents of the text file into a string. The string will contain valid JSON encoded data.

2. Next, we call `JsonConvert.DeserializeObject<>` to construct a .NET object from the string:

    ```
    string poiString = File.ReadAllText (filename);
    PointOfInterest poi = JsonConvert.DeserializeObject<PointOfIntere
      st> (poiString);
    ```

To load the cache, we need to obtain a directory of all the `*.json` files and load each POI into the cache. The following listing demonstrates how to accomplish this using the `Directory` class from `System.IO`:

```
public void RefreshCache()
{
   _pois.Clear ();
```

```
string[] filenames = Directory.GetFiles (_storagePath, "*.json");

foreach (string filename in filenames) {
  string poiString = File.ReadAllText (filename);
  PointOfInterest poi = JsonConvert.DeserializeObject<PointOfIntere
    st> (poiString);
  _pois.Add (poi);
}
}
```

Implementing SavePOI()

SavePOI() will be called to save the new and existing POIs, so it fulfils two of the CRUD functions, create and update. In the case of a new POI, SavePOI() needs to assign a value to Id. As you may recall from earlier in the chapter, we can determine whether a POI is new by checking if it has a null ID.

When assigning a new ID, we will take a very simplistic approach. We will inspect the cache of the POIs to determine the highest Id and increment it by 1 to get the next Id.

Create a private method named GetNextId(), which returns an integer based on the logic previously described. The following code snippet is from the code bundle of this book. You will need to use the System.Linq namespace.

```
private int GetNextId()

  {

  if (_pois.Count == 0)

    return 1;

  else

    return _pois.Max (p => p.Id.Value) + 1;

  }
```

We need to create one more supporting method to determine the filename. Create a private method named GetFilename(), which accepts an integer ID and returns a string containing the filename. The following code snippet is from the code bundle of this book:

```
private string GetFilename(int id)
{
   return Path.Combine(_storagePath,"poi" + id.ToString() + ".json");
}
```

Note the use of `Path.Combine()` to build the path. This ensures that the proper delimiter is used to construct the path based on the platform on which the code is being executed.

We will now turn our attention to the main logic in `SavePOI()`. Let's consider how we take a .NET object and store it in a JSON-formatted text file using Json.NET, essentially just the opposite of what we accomplished in the `RefreshCache()` method. The process in reverse is just as easy.

1. Convert the .NET object to a JSON string using `JsonConvert.SerializeObject()`.

2. Save the string to a text file:

    ```
    string poiString = JsonConvert.SerializeObject (poi);
    File.WriteAllText (GetFilename (poi.Id), poiString);
    ```

Now it is just a matter of putting all of these pieces together in the `SavePOI()` method. The following code snippet is from the code bundle of this book:

```
public void SavePOI (PointOfInterest poi)
{
   Boolean newPOI = false;
   if (!poi.Id.HasValue) {
     poi.Id = GetNextId ();
     newPOI = true;
   }

   // serialize POI
   string poiString = JsonConvert.SerializeObject (poi);
   // write new file or overwrite existing file
   File.WriteAllText (GetFilename (poi.Id.Value), poiString);

   // update cache if file save was successful
   if (newPOI)
     _pois.Add (poi);
}
```

Note that we only need to add a POI to the cache when creating a new one and only after successfully writing the file.

Implementing GetPOI()

GetPOI() is a simple method to implement since we have a cache. We simply need to use the Find method on the _poi list and return the results. You will need to use System.Linq. The following code snippet is from the code bundle of this book:

```
public PointOfInterest GetPOI (int id)
{
    PointOfInterest poi = _pois.Find (p => p.Id == id);
    return poi;
}
```

Run POITestApp and execute the tests. The test for CreatePOI() and UpdatePOI() should now be executed successfully.

Implementing DeletePOI()

DeletePOI() is also relatively simple. File.Delete() can be used to delete the file and, when successful, we need to be sure to remove the POI from the cache. The following code is from the code bundle of this book:

```
public void DeletePOI (PointOfInterest poi)
{
  File.Delete (GetFilename (poi.Id));
  _pois.Remove (poi);
}
```

Run POITestApp and execute the tests. Everything should run successfully now.

Summary

In this chapter, we have created a JSON-based storage service for our POI data and created a series of unit tests to verify whether the service is functioning. In the next chapter, we begin to develop the user interface by creating a list view with a search/filtering capability.

5
Adding a List View

In this chapter, we finally get to what many of you have been waiting for, developing the user interface. We will walk through the activities related to creating and populating a list view, which includes the following topics:

- The `ListView` and `ListAdapter` classes
- Creating the Points of Interest `list view` layout
- Extending `BaseAdapter<>` to provide data to the `ListView` widget
- Creating a custom cell layout
- Handling row selections

Creating the POI ListView layout

When we created the `POIApp` project, a default layout and activity was created for us. Rather than deleting these, let's give them more appropriate names and remove unnecessary content as follows:

1. Select `main.axml` in **Resources** | **Layout**.
2. Right-click on it, select **Rename**, and enter the name as `POIList.axml`.
3. Double-click on it to open `POIList.axml`.
4. Click on the **Hello World** button and then click on the the **Delete** button.
5. Select `MainActivity.cs` and rename it as `POIListActivity.cs`.
6. Double-click on it to open `POIListActivity.cs`.
7. Rename the class inside as `POIListActivity`.
8. Change the layout ID referenced in the `SetContentView()` API call to `Resources.Layout.POIList`.

9. Remove the code related to the **Hello World** button that we removed from the layout. Your class should now look like the following code:

```
[Activity (Label = "POIs", MainLauncher = true)]
public class POIListActivity : Activity
{
  protected override void OnCreate (Bundle bundle)
  {
    base.OnCreate (bundle);

    SetContentView (Resource.Layout.POIList);
  }
}
```

Now, we need to add a ListView widget from the **Toolbox** pad. By default the **Toolbox** pad is displayed on the top right-hand side of the IDE as follows:

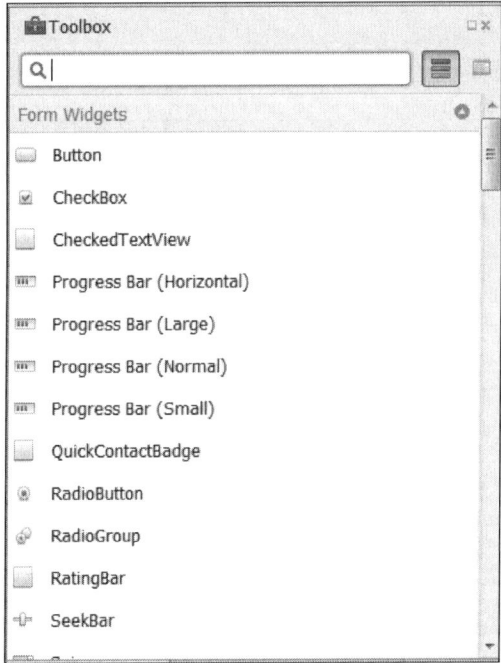

The **Toolbox** pad is organized with basic widgets at the top of the list and container widgets such as ListViews further down the list. There is a search box at the top that allows you to filter the widgets in the list, and there are two buttons to the right-hand side of the search box that allow you to adjust the way widgets are listed. Now, perform the following steps:

1. Enter `ListView` in the search field.

2. Select the `ListView` widget, drag it over the content area of the layout designer, and drop it on the layout.

You have now added a `ListView` widget to `POIList.axml`. On the bottom right-hand side of the IDE, you will notice the **Properties** and **Document Outline** pads.

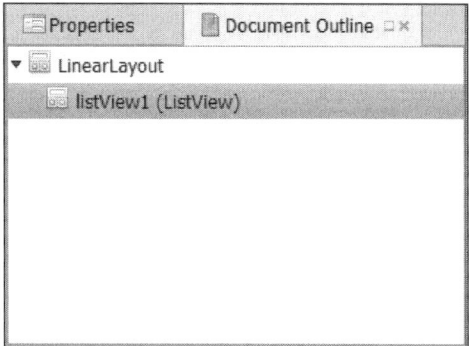

Activate the **Document Outline** pad and you will see an outline of your layout document listing all the widgets, Views, or view groups contained in it. The **Document Outline** pad provides a convenient means of navigating and selecting widgets, particularly as layouts get more complex. Select `listView1` and then click on the **Properties** tab.

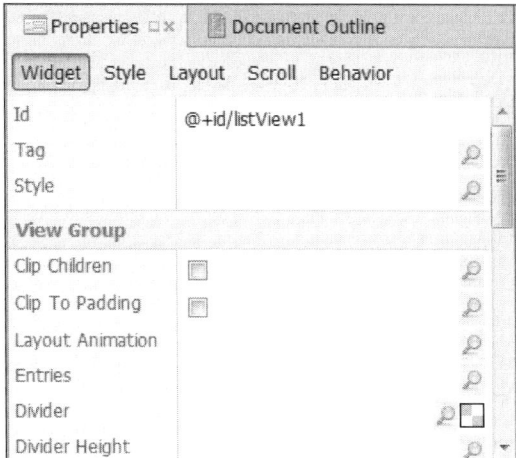

The **Properties** pad allows you to modify the properties of the currently selected widget. There are five buttons at the top of the pad that switch the set of properties being edited. As you may recall from *Chapter 1, The Anatomy of an Android App*, the @+id notation notifies the compiler that a new resource ID needs to be created to identify the widget in API calls, and listView1 identifies the name of the constant. Now, perform the following steps:

1. Change the ID name to poiListView and save the changes.
2. Switch back to the **Document Outline** pad and note the changed name.
3. Switch back to the **Properties** pad and click on the **Layout** button.
4. Under the **View Group** section of the layout properties; note that the width is set to match_parent. Enter the same setting for the height. This simply tells the control that it can use the entire content area provided by the parent, excluding any margins specified. In our case, the parent would be the top-level LinearLayout.

> Prior to API level 8, fill_parent was used instead of match_parent to accomplish the same effect. In API level 8, fill_parent was deprecated and replaced with match_parent for clarity. Currently, both the constants are defined as the same value, so they have exactly the same effect. However, fill_parent may be removed from the future releases of the API; so, going forward, match_parent should be used.

Now let's focus on the layout designer. You will notice two buttons, **Content** and **Source**, at the bottom of the designer, which allow you to switch between a visual representation of the layout (**Content**) and an XML source code view of the layout (**Source**). This is very useful as some tasks are just quicker in the Source view; however, the Content view is useful in viewing the arrangement of widgets visually. The Content view's usefulness is somewhat limited only because many times portions of a view must be constructed with code at runtime; however, when the view can be specified completely in XML, the Content view is very useful.

In the Content view, you will notice a few useful tools arranged at the top of the window, as shown in the following screenshot:

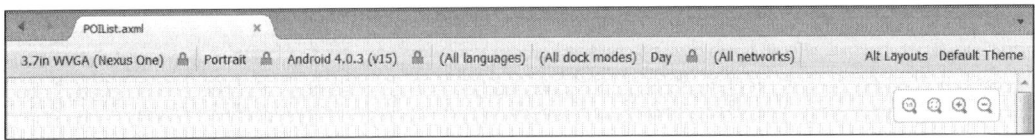

In the upper-right corner, you will find a set of zooming controls. These allow you to zoom the layout in or out depending on your monitor size and the level of details you would like to view. Across the top, you will find drop-down menus that also let you select things such as the screen size of the device to simulate, orientation of the device, and the version of the Android platform to simulate.

We now turn our attention to the layout for each row in the `ListView` widget. The Android platform provides a number of default layouts that can be used with a `ListView` widget.

Layout	Description
SimpleListItem1	A single line with a single caption field.
SimpleListItem2	A two-line layout with a larger font and a brighter text color for the first field.
TwoLineListItem	A two-line layout with an equal sized font for both lines and a brighter text color for the first line.
ActivityListItem	A single line of text with an image view.

For more control over content layout, a custom layout can also be created, which is what is needed for `poiListView`.

To create a new layout, perform the following steps:

1. In the **Solution** pad, select **Resources | Layout**, right-click on it, and select **Add | New File**.

2. Select **Android** from the list on the left-hand side, **Android Layout** from the template list, enter `POIListItem` in the name column, and click on **New**.

There are a number of ways to achieve this layout, but we will go with a `RelativeLayout` utility to demonstrate its capabilities. The following diagram shows the way the POI data should be organized:

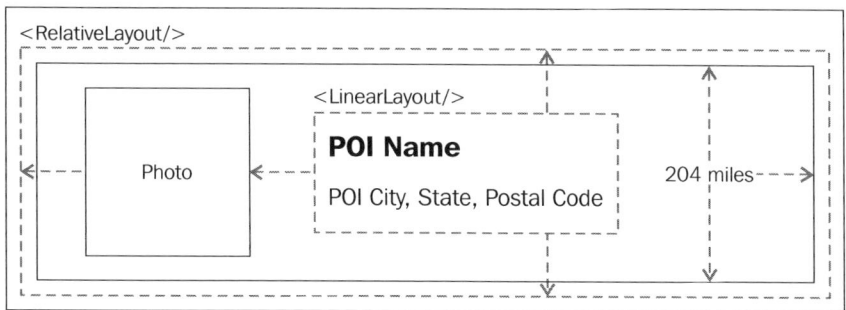

There is a lot going on in this diagram. Let's break it down as follows:

- A `RelativeLayout` view group is used as the top-level container; it provides a number of flexible options for positioning a relative content, its edges, or other content.

- An `ImageView` widget is used to display a photo of the POI, and it is anchored to the left-hand side of the `RelativeLayout` utility.

- Two `TextView` widgets are used to display the POI name and address information. They need to be anchored to the right-hand side of the `ImageView` widget and centered within the parent `RelativeLayout` utility. The easiest way to accomplish this is to place both `TextView` classes inside another layout; in this case, a `LinearLayout` widget with the orientation set to vertical.

- An additional `TextView` widget is used to display the distance, and it is anchored on the right-hand side of the `RelativeLayout` view group and centered vertically.

Now, our task is to get this definition into `POIListItem.axml`. The next few sections describe how to accomplish this using the `Content` view of the designer when feasible and the `Source` view when required.

Adding a RelativeLayout view group

When `POIListItem.axml` was created, a top-level `LinearLayout` was added. Change this top-level `ViewGroup` drawable to be a `RelativeLayout` view group:

1. With `POIListItem.axml` opened in the content mode, select the entire layout by clicking on the content area. You should see a blue outline going around the edge.

2. Press **Delete**. The `LinearLayout` view group will be deleted and you will see a message indicating that the layout is empty.

3. Locate the `RelativeLayout` view group in the toolbox and drag it onto the layout.

4. With the `RelativeLayout` view group selected, use the **Properties** pad to set the **Padding** option to `5dp`, the **Layout Height** option to `wrap_content`, and the **Layout Width** option to `match_parent`. The padding controls how much space will be placed around each `ListView` item as a margin, and the height determines how much of the `parent` control height is used. The **Padding** and **Layout Height** values can be set from the **Layout** section of the **Properties** pad.

Setting the **Layout Width** option to match_ parent will cause the POIListItem content to consume the entire width of the screen, while setting the **Layout Height** option to wrap_content will cause each row to be equal to the longest control; in this case, it is the ImageView widget.

Android runs on a variety of devices that offer different screen sizes and densities. When specifying dimensions, you can use a number of different units including **pixels (px)**, **inches (in)**, and **density-independent pixels (dp)**. Density-independent pixels are abstract units based on 1 dp being 1 pixel on a 160 dpi screen. At runtime, Android will scale the actual size up or down based on the actual screen density. It is best practice to specify dimensions using density-independent pixels.

Adding an ImageView widget

Add an ImageView widget to the left-hand side of the layout to display an image if available for the POI as follows:

1. Locate the ImageView widget in the toolbox and drag it onto the layout.

2. With the ImageView widget selected, use the **Properties** pad to set the name to poiImageView, and the height and width to 65dp. The name can be set from the **Widget** section of the **Properties** pad, and the **Height** and **Width** options from the **Layout** section.

3. In the property grouping named RelativeLayout, set **Center Vertical** to true. Simply clicking on the checkbox does not seem to work, but you can click on the small icon that looks like an edit box to the right-hand side and just enter true. If everything else fails, just switch to the Source view and enter the following code line:

```
android:layout_centerVertical="true"
```

Adding a LinearLayout widget

Add a LinearLayout view group that will be used to lay out the POI name and address data as follows:

1. Locate the **LinearLayout (vertical)** view group in the toolbox. Adding this widget is a little trickier because we want it anchored to the right-hand side of the ImageView widget. Drag the LinearLayout view group to the right-hand side of the ImageView widget until the edge turns to a blue dashed line, and then drop the LinearLayout view group. It will be aligned with the right-hand side of the ImageView widget.

2. In the property grouping named **RelativeLayout** of the **Layout** section, set **Center Vertical** to `true`. As before, you will need to enter `true` in the edit box or manually add it in the `Source` view.

3. Switch to the **Code** view to see what has been added to the layout. Notice the following code lines from the listing:

```
android:layout_toRightOf="@id/poiImageView"
android:layout_centerVertical="true"
```

Adding the name and address TextView classes

Add `TextView` classes to display the POI name and address:

1. Locate `TextView` in the toolbox and add a `TextView` to the layout. This `TextView` needs to be added within the `LinearLayout` view group we just added, so drag `TextView` over the `LinearLayout` view group until it turns blue and drop it.

2. Name the `TextView` as `nameTextView` and set the text size to `22sp`. The text size can be set in the **Style** section of the **Properties** pad; you will need to expand the **Text Appearance** group by clicking on the ellipsis button on the right-hand side.

 Scale-independent Pixels (sp) are like dp units, but they are also scaled by the user's font size preference. Android allows users to select a font size in the **Accessibility** section of **Settings**. When font sizes are specified using sp, Android will not only take into account the screen density when scaling text, but will also consider the user's accessibility settings. It is recommended you specify font sizes using sp.

3. Change the sample text in `nameTextView` to `POI Name`. This can be accomplished by double-clicking on the widget in the **Content** view and entering the text directly. Alternately, it can be entered in the **Widget** section of the **Properties** pad.

4. Add another `TextView` to the `LinearLayout` view group using the same technique except dragging the new widget to the bottom edge of the `nameTextView` until it changes to a blue dashed line and dropping it. This will cause the second `TextView` to be added below `nameTextView`. Set the font size to `14sp`.

5. Name the new `TextView` as `addrTextView` and set the sample text to **City, State, Postal Code**.

Adding the Distance TextView

Add a `TextView` to show the distance from POI:

1. Locate the `TextView` in the toolbox and add a `TextView` to the layout. This `TextView` needs to be anchored to the right-hand side of the `RelativeLayout` view group, but there is no way to visually accomplish this; so, we will use a multistep process. Initially, align the `TextView` with the left-hand edge of the `LinearLayout` view group by dragging it to the left-hand side until the edge changes to a dashed blue line and drop it.

2. In the **Widget** section of the **Properties** pad, name the widget as `distanceTextView` and set the font size to `14sp`.

3. In the **Layout** section of the **Properties** pad, set **Align Parent Right** to `true`, **Center Vertical** to `true`, and clear out the `linearLayout1` view group name in the **To Right Of** layout property. Change the sample text to `204 miles`.

The following diagram depicts what should be seen from the `Content` view at this point:

Populating the ListView item

There are a number of ways to populate a `ListView` item within the Android platform; they all work with some type of adapter, meaning a subtype of `BaseAdapter` or some type of class that implements the `IListAdapter` interface. For simple lists, you will commonly see the use of `ArrayAdapter<T>`.

We will create a subtype of `BaseAdapter<T>` as it meets our specific need, works well in many scenarios, and allows for the use of our custom layout.

Shared instance of IPOIDataService

Prior to creating the adapter, we need to consider how we will get access to an instance of the data service since it will be the source of our POI data. As you may recall from *Chapter 4, Creating a Data Storage Mechanism*, we simply created an instance within the test fixture. That worked fine for testing; however, in the POIApp project, we need a single instance that we can use throughout the app, meaning each activity and view needs to share the same instance of the data service. There are many ways to accomplish this; for our purposes, we can create a class that houses a single static field that is an instance of IPOIDataService. The following code demonstrates this approach:

```
public class POIData
{
  public static readonly IPOIDataService Service = new
    POIJsonService(
    Path.Combine(
      Android.OS.Environment.ExternalStorageDirectory.Path,
    "POIApp"));
}
```

Note that in this example, we used the Android.OS.Environment class to get the path for the external storage directory. This is a storage location different from the one we used in POITestApp. We are now using the external storage directory for the following reasons:

1. The external storage directory will not be automatically deleted when our app is uninstalled; as we develop our app, we will not face a risk of losing data if we need to uninstall the app. For POITestApp, it was advantageous to always have the data removed.

2. While running on a physical device, it is much easier to access the external storage directory to copy files to and from than access an apps data directory, which is secured.

3. Directories inside the external storage directory can be accessed by other apps. In *Chapter 8, Adding Camera App Integration*, we will add integration with a camera app, and using the external storage directory means we can have the camera app store our picture for us.

Create the POIData class or an equivalent implementation.

Permissions

Android apps must be granted permissions to accomplish certain tasks. One of these tasks is writing to the external storage directory. You specify permissions that an app requires in the `AndroidManifest.xml` file. This allows the installer to show potential users the set of permissions an app requires at install time.

To set the appropriate permissions, perform the following steps:

1. Double-click on `AndroidManifest.xml` from **Properties** in the **Solution** pad. The file will be open in the manifest editor. There are two tabs, **Application** and **Source**, at the bottom of the screen, which can be used to toggle between viewing a form for editing the file and the raw XML, as shown in the following screenshot:

2. In the **Required permissions** list, check `WRITE_EXTERNAL_STORAGE` and navigate to **File | Save**.

3. Switch to the `Source` view to view the XML as follows:

```
AndroidManifest.xml

1 <?xml version="1.0" encoding="utf-8"?>
2 <manifest xmlns:android="http://schemas.android.com/apk/res/android"
3         android:versionCode="1" android:versionName="1.0" package="POIApp">
4     <uses-sdk />
5     <application android:label="POIApp" android:icon="@drawable/ic_app">
6     </application>
7     <uses-permission android:name="android.permission.WRITE_EXTERNAL_STORAGE" />
8 </manifest>
```

Creating POIListViewAdapter

In order to create POIListViewAdapter, start by creating a custom adapter as follows:

1. Create a new class named `POIListViewAdapter`.

2. Open the class file, make the class a public class, and specify that it inherits from `BaseAdapter<PointOfInterest>`.

Now that the adapter class has been created, we need to provide a constructor and implement four abstract methods.

Implementing a constructor

We need to implement a constructor that will accept all the information we will need to work with to populate the list. Typically, you will at least need two parameters passed in; an `Activity` parameter, because we need to use some of its services to create our custom list view, and some form of list that can be enumerated to populate the `ListView` item. In our case, we have a global reference to the data service we created, which caches POIs, so we only need a single parameter, an `Activity` parameter. The following code shows the constructor from the code bundle:

```
private readonly Activity _context;

public POIListViewAdapter(Activity context)
{
  _context = context;
}
```

Implementing Count { get; }

The `BaseAdapter<T>` class provides an abstract definition for a read-only `Count` property. In our case, we simply need to provide the count of POIs that we have in our cache. The following code example demonstrates the implementation from the code bundle:

```
public override int Count
{
  get { return POIData.Service.POIs.Count; }
}
```

Implementing GetItemId()

The `BaseAdapter<T>` class provides an abstract definition for a method that returns an `int` ID for a row in the data source. We can use the `position` parameter to access a POI in the cache and return the corresponding ID. The following code example demonstrates the implementation from the code bundle:

```
public override long GetItemId(int position)
{
   Return POIData.Service.POIs[position].Id.Value;
}
```

Implementing the index getter method

The `BaseAdapter<T>` class provides an abstract definition for an index getter method that returns a typed object based on a `position` parameter passed in as an index. We can use the `position` parameter to access the POI in the cache and return an instance. The following code example demonstrates the implementation from the code bundle:

```
public override PointOfInterest this[int position]
{
   get { return POIData.Service.POIs[position]; }
}
```

Implementing GetView()

The `BaseAdapter<T>` class provides an abstract definition for `GetView()`, which returns a view instance that represents a single row in the `ListView` item. As in other scenarios, you can choose to construct the view entirely in code or to construct it from a layout file. We will use the layout file we previously created. The following code example demonstrates "inflating" a view from a layout file:

```
var view =
   _context.LayoutInflater.Inflate(Resource.Layout.POIListItem,
      null);
```

The first parameter of `Inflate` is a resource ID and the second is a root `ViewGroup`, which in this case can be left `null` since the view will be added to the `ListView` item when it is returned.

Reusing row Views

The `GetView()` method is called for each row in the source dataset. For datasets with large numbers of rows, hundreds or even thousands, it would require a great deal of resources to create a separate view for each row and it would seem wasteful since only a few rows are visible at any given time. The `AdapterView` architecture addresses this need by placing row Views into a queue that can be reused as they scroll out of view of the user. The `GetView()` method accepts a parameter named `convertView`, which is of type `View`. When a view is available for reuse, `convertView` will contain a reference to the view; otherwise, it will be `null` and a new view should be created. The following code example has depicted the use of `convertView` to facilitate the reuse of row Views:

```
View view = convertView;
if (view == null)
view =
  _context.LayoutInflater.Inflate(Resource.Layout.POIListItem,
    null);
```

Populating row Views

Now that we have an instance of the view, we need to populate the fields. The `View` class defines a named `FindViewById<T>` method, which returns a typed instance of a widget contained in the view. You pass in the resource ID defined in the layout file to specify the control you wish to access. The following code returns access to the `nameTextView` and sets the `Text` property:

```
PointOfInterest poi = POIData.Service.POIs [position];

view.FindViewById<TextView>
(Resource.Id.nameTextView).Text = poi.Name;
```

Populating `addrTextView` is slightly more complicated because we only want to use the portions of the address we have, and we want to hide the `TextView` if none of the address components are present.

The `View.Visibility` property allows for controlling whether a view is visible or not. It is based on the `ViewStates` enum, which defines the following values:

Value	Description
Gone	Tells the parent `ViewGroup` to treat `View` as though it does not exist, so no space will be allocated in the layout.
Invisible	Tells the parent `ViewGroup` to hide the content for the `View`.

Value	Description
Visible	Tells the parent `ViewGroup` to display the content of the `View`.

In our case, we want to use the `Gone` value if none of the components of the address are present. The following code shows the logic in the `GetView`:

```
if (String.IsNullOrEmpty (poi.Address))
  view.FindViewById<TextView>
  (Resource.Id.addrTextView).Visibility = ViewStates.Gone;
else
  view.FindViewById<TextView>
  (Resource.Id.addrTextView).Text = poi.Address;
```

Hooking up POIListViewAdapter

The last task related to the adapter is hooking it up to the `ListView` item. We need to switch back to the `POIListActivity` class and add the following declarations:

```
ListView _poiListView;
POIListViewAdapter _adapter;
```

Now, within the `OnCreate` method, we need to create an instance of `POIListViewAdapter` and connect it to the `Listview` item. The following code is from the code bundle:

```
protected override void OnCreate (Bundle bundle)
{
  base.OnCreate (bundle);

  SetContentView (Resource.Layout.POIList);

  _poiListView = FindViewById<ListView>
  (Resource.Id.poiListView);
  _adapter = new POIListViewAdapter (this);
  _poiListView.Adapter = _adapter;
}
```

Adding actions to ActionBar

Android apps have access to add activity-specific actions to the `ActionBar` at the top of the device screen, just below the status bar. We will define two actions for the `POIListActivity` class; `New`, to create a new POI, and `Refresh`, to refresh the cache of POIs from the device's local storage.

The `Activity` class provides the following virtual methods that can be overridden to add actions:

Virtual Method	Description
OnCreateOptionsMenu	It allows for the creation of the actions either through API calls or through inflating an XML definition.
OnOptionsItemSelected	It is called when an action in the `ActionBar` is clicked.

Defining the menu .xml file

Actions can be defined in a menu XML file that resides in the `Resources/menu` folder, or it can be created programmatically using API calls. We will define the New and Refresh actions in an XML file named `POIListViewMenu.xml`.

To create `POIListViewMenu.xml`, perform the following steps:

1. Select the `Resources` folder in `POIApp`, right-click on it and click on **Add | New Folder**.

2. Name the folder `menu`.

3. Select the `menu` folder, right-click on it and click on **Add | New File**.

4. Select **XML | Empty XML File**, enter `POIListViewMenu.xml` for the name and click on **New**.

You now need to fill in the definitions for the two actions we identified. Unfortunately, Xamarin Studio does not contain a template for menu XML files, so you have to hunt the format down from Android documentation or online examples. The following code contains definitions for `actionNew` and `actionRefresh`:

```
<menu xmlns:android="http://schemas.android.com/apk/res/android">
  <item android:id="@+id/actionNew"
    android:icon="@drawable/ic_new"
    android:title="New"
  android:showAsAction="ifRoom" />
  <item android:id="@+id/actionRefresh"
    android:icon="@drawable/ic_refresh"
    android:title="Refresh"
  android:showAsAction="ifRoom" />
</menu>
```

Note that from the menu definition, we have referenced two new drawables; `ic_new` and `ic_refresh`. We need to add these images to the project the same way that we did for the `ic_app` icon in *Chapter 3, Creating the Points of Interest App*. The images can be found in the `drawable` folder present in the assets location.

Setting menus in OnCreateOptionsMenu()

The OnCreateOptionsMenu() method is called to give an opportunity to the Activity parameter to define actions for the ActionBar. The Activity class provides a MenuInflater method, which reads the XML definition file and places the action defined on the ActionBar. The following code shows the implementation from
the code bundle:

```
public override bool OnCreateOptionsMenu(IMenu menu)
{
  MenuInflater.Inflate(Resource.Menu.poiListViewMenu, menu);
  return base.OnCreateOptionsMenu(menu);
}
```

Handling selection in OnOptionsItemSelected()

The OnOptionsItemSelected() method is called whenever an action in the ActionBar is clicked and an instance of IMenuItem is passed in. The IMenuItem.ItemId instance corresponds to the ID specified in the item definition and can be used to determine which action was clicked on. The following code shows the implementation of OnOptionsItemSelected() from the code bundle:

```
public override bool OnOptionsItemSelected (IMenuItem item)
{
  switch (item.ItemId)
  {
    case Resource.Id.actionNew:
    // place holder for creating new poi
    return true;

    case Resource.Id.actionRefresh:
    POIData.Service.RefreshCache ();
    _adapter.NotifyDataSetChanged ();
    return true;

    default :
    return base.OnOptionsItemSelected(item);
  }
}
```

Note that we have simply created a placeholder for `actionNew` and placed two method calls for `actionRefresh`.

The `POIJsonService.RefreshCache()` method is called to refresh the cache with the `*.json` files stored locally on the device.

The `_adapter.NotifyDataSetChanged` method is called so that `poiListView` will be refreshed based on the updated cache of POIs.

Configuring an SD card for the emulator

If using the emulator for development, you will need to configure it to have an SD card for storing the POI data.

To configure an SD card for the emulator, perform the following steps:

1. From the main menu, navigate to **Tools | Open Android Emulator Manager**.
2. Select the emulator you have been working with and click on **Edit**.
3. At the bottom of the **Edit AVD** dialog box, you will see the **SD Card** section. Click on **Size**, enter `1023` in the edit box and select **MiB** from the drop-down menu on the right-hand side. Click on **OK** to save.

Running POIApp

We have done a great deal of work so far, now it's time to compile and run the app. Compile and run the application using the Android emulator based on the procedure we used in the previous chapters.

You will probably be disappointed to see an empty screen after all that work. Obviously, the issue is that we do not have any data to display, and we have not yet created the features that allow us to create new data. Bummer!

The next section discusses how to use the Android Device Monitor to push files to an emulator or device so that we can see some data in our app. Leave the app running in the emulator and go through the next section.

Android Device Monitor

The Android SDK ships with the **Android Device Monitor (ADM)** app, which is packed with features that help you develop and debug your app either while it is running in an emulator or on a device. The Android Device Monitor supersedes the **Dalvik Debug Monitor Service (DDMS)** app, which provides similar capabilities. In this section, we will look at how we can use ADM to manage files.

First, let's add a menu item under the **Tools** menu in Xamarin Studio for easy access by performing the following steps:

1. Select **Tools | Options**.

2. Under the **Environment** section, click on **External Tools** and then click on **Add**.

3. Enter `Android Device Monitor` for the title.

4. Click on the **Browse** action for the command, navigate to **Tools** under the SDK location, select `Android Device monitor.bat` and click on **Open**. The SDK location can be determined by clicking on **SDK Locations | Android** in the **Options** dialog box.

To copy files to an emulator or device, perform the following steps:

1. Start ADM by selecting the newly created **Tools** menu item. When ADM starts, you will see currently running emulators and connect devices listed on the left-hand side of the window.

2. Select the emulator instance or connected device you would like to work with.

3. Select the **File Explorer** tab on the right-hand side of the window. If the **File Explorer** tab is not visible, select **Window | Show View** from the main menu and click on **File Explorer**.

4. Navigate to `/storage/sdcard/POIApp`. There should be no files listed under the folder. While working with actual devices rather than emulators, the physical folder to navigate to may not be obvious due to various mounts that may be in place. For example, the actual location on my HTC One, `/mnt/shell/emulated/0`. ADM will display mounts to the right-hand side of each folder listed as follows:

▼ 📂 storage	2013-11-13	19:36	d---r-x---
▼ 📂 emulated	2013-11-13	19:36	dr-xr-xr-x
📂 legacy	2013-11-13	19:36	lrwxrwxrwx -> /mnt/shell/emulated/0
📂 sdcard0	2013-11-13	19:36	lrwxrwxrwx -> /storage/emulated/legacy
▶ 📂 usb	2013-11-13	19:36	d---------
▶ 📂 sys	2013-11-13	19:36	dr-xr-xr-x

5. Click on the `Push` file onto the **Device** button in the upper-right corner of the tab. Navigate to the `data` folder in the assets location, select `poi1.json`, and click on **Open**.

6. Repeat step 5 for each `*.json` file in the `data` folder.

7. Switch back to the Android emulator and click on the **Refresh** action in `POIApp`. You should now see the POIs listed.

The files that we uploaded from the assets folder are simple text files encoded using JSON. The JSON specifications can be viewed at www.json.org. We will not cover the JSON specifications in this book, but you can create additional JSON files using any text editor and using the existing files as templates.

Handling row clicks

When a user clicks on a row, the POI app will navigate to a detailed view to allow viewing and updating of the complete set of information. We will build the detailed view in the next chapter but will go ahead and discuss handling clicks now. Clicks can be handled using a traditional event handler. The ListView item provides an ItemClick event handler, which accepts a ListView.ItemClickEventArgs parameter. The ListView.ItemClickEventArgs parameter provides the following information that can be used for processing the event:

Property	Description
Id	It is the ID for the data associated with the row that was clicked. This would be the value returned from GetItemId().
Position	It is the position in the ListView item of the row that was clicked.
View	It is the view associated with the row that was clicked. This would be the view returned from GetView().
Parent	It is the AdapterView architecture that contains the row that was clicked. In our case, it is ListView.

Create an event handler in POIListActivity for processing click events on the ListView item. We are not ready to add the navigation since we have not yet created our detailed view, so we will just write a line out to the console showing which POI was clicked. The following code is from the code bundle:

```
protected void POIClicked(object sender,
  ListView.ItemClickEventArgs e)
{
  PointOfInterest poi = POIDataService.GetPOI ((int)e.Id);
  Console.WriteLine ("POIClicked: Name is {0}", poi.Name);
}
```

We also need to hook up the event handler. Add the following line of code to the end of the OnCreate method:

```
_poiListView.ItemClick += POIClicked;
```

Run the POIApp project and click on a POI; switch to Xamarin Studio to view the **Application Output** pad.

Summary

In this chapter, we have covered the details of creating and populating a list view. In the next chapter, we will add a detailed view to POIApp.

6

Adding a Detail View

In this chapter, we will walk through creating a detailed view for displaying, updating, and deleting POIs. The following topics will be covered:

- Creating the POIDetail layout and activity
- Binding variables to user interface widgets
- Navigating between activities
- Passing data with the Intent class
- Adding validation and using EditText.Error to display error messages
- Displaying confirmation prompts
- Displaying toasts

Creating the POIDetail layout

We will start by creating a new layout:

1. Select the Resources/Layout folder in the **Solution** pad.
2. Right-click on **Add** and select **New File**.
3. In the **New File** dialog, click on **Android** and select **Android Layout**, enter POIDetail in the **Name** field, and select **New**.

   By default, layouts are created with LinearLayout as the top-level container. The POIDetail view will have a number of fields and will likely require scrolling on most devices. The POIList layout gave us scrolling for free because we were using ListView; however, in the case of POIDetail, we will need to use ScrollView.

4. With the POIDetail.xaml file opened in the Content view, select the top-level **Linear Layout** and press the *Delete* key.

5. In the **Toolbox** pad, locate the **ScrollView** widget and drag it onto the Content View.

6. In the **Toolbox** pad, locate the **LinearLayout (vertical)** widget and drag it onto the Content View inside ScrollView.

7. With LinearLayout selected, set **Padding** in the **Layout** section of the **Properties** pad to **5dp**.

We are now ready to add field labels and edit controls to the layout. The following screenshot depicts the layout we are trying to achieve:

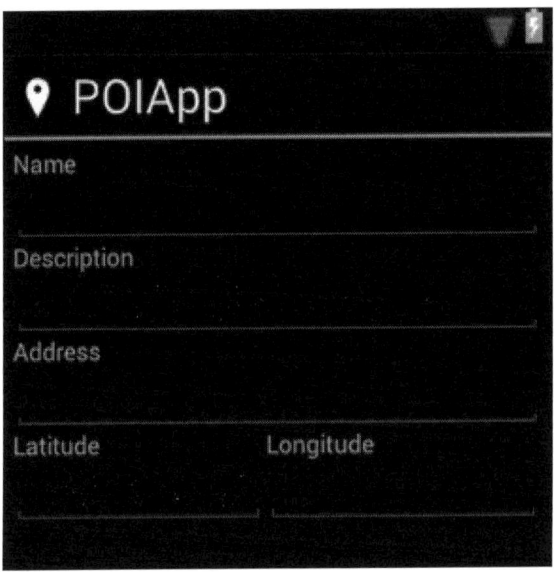

We will use simple TextView widgets to serve as labels and EditText widgets to serve as input controls. The EditText widget contains a number of properties that can be used to customize its behavior. One of these properties is named InputType, and it controls aspects such as which type of keyboard to use for inputs (Alpha, Numeric, and so on) and how many lines of text are allowed. The **Toolbox** pad presents a number of templates or preconfigured EditText widgets in the list under the group name **Text Fields**. The following screenshot depicts the list:

Add a series of `TextView` and `EditText` controls for the **Name**, **Description**, and **Address** fields. Name the `EditText` widgets according to the following table and use the corresponding **Toolbox** widget so that the appropriate editing characteristics are applied:

Name	Widget toolbox name
nameEditText	Plain Text
descrEditText	Multiline Text
addrEditText	Multiline Text

We are now ready to address the **Latitude** and **Longitude** fields, and we will employ a new layout manager, TableLayout. We would like to see these fields depicted in a table with two rows and two columns with the top row being used for the labels and the bottom row being used for the edit fields. In order to do so, perform the following steps:

1. Locate TableLayout in the **Toolbox** pad, drag it onto the Content View below the addrEditText widget and drop it. A TableLayout will be created with three rows and three columns.

2. Select one of the rows in TableLayout, right-click on and select **Delete Row**.

3. Select one of the columns in the TableLayout, right-click on and select **Delete Column**.

4. Select the first column, right-click on and select **Stretch Column**. Similarly, do it for the second column.

You should now have a TableLayout with a visible outline of two rows, each having two columns like what is depicted in the following screenshot:

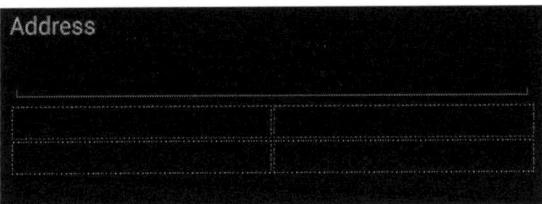

We now need to add TextView widgets for the two labels in the first row and **Number (decimal)** widgets for the **Latitude** and **Longitude** edit controls, naming them latEditText and longEditText.

We have now completed the POIDetail.xaml layout, and the Content View you see should look the same as the previous diagram.

Working with InputType

The EditText element provides a property named InputType that checks the behavior of the control when data is being entered. When the description and address widgets were added, we selected **Multiline Text** from the **Toolbox** pad. The following code shows that in this case the input type was automatically set:

```
<EditText
   p1:inputType="textMultiLine"
   p1:layout_width="fill_parent"
   p1:layout_height="wrap_content"
   p1:id="@+id/descrEditText" />
```

The `InputType` property can also be set or changed from within the **Properties** pad under the **Widget** tab in the **Input Format** section. What may not be obvious is that **Input Type** can combine values, which come in handy in our situation. The following table shows a reasonable set of values for **Input Type**; feel free to experiment:

Widget	Input Type
`nameEditText`	`inputType="textCapWords"`
`descrEditText`	`inputType="textMultiLine|textCapSentences"`
`addrEditText`	`inputType="textMultiLine"`
`latEditText`	`inputType="numberDecimal|numberSigned"`
`longEditText`	`inputType="numberDecimal|numberSigned"`

Creating POIDetailActivity

Now that we have the layout complete, we need a corresponding activity. To create `POIDetailActivity`, perform the following steps:

1. With the `POIApp` project selected in the **Solution** pad, right-click on it and navigate to **Add | New File**.

2. From the **New File** dialog, click on **Android** and select **Android Activity**, enter `POIDetailActivity` as **Name**, and click on **New**.

As you may recall from the last chapter, one of the first things that need to be done when an activity is created is to set the content, which is accomplished with a call to `SetContentView()`. Add the following line of code to the `OnCreate()` method of the new activity:

```
SetContentView (Resource.Layout.POIDetail);
```

Binding variables to controls

As we learned in the previous chapter, we need to manually bind user interface widgets to internal program references in order to manipulate their content, assign event handlers, and so on. Declare a set of private variables for each of the input widgets we created in the layout. The following listing is from the source folder:

```
EditText _nameEditText;
EditText _descrEditText;
EditText _addrEditText;
EditText _latEditText;
EditText _longEditText;
ImageView _poiImageView;
```

A call to `FindViewById<T>` is required to bind each variable to its corresponding user interface widget. The following listing depicts what should be added to the `OnCreate()` method somewhere after the call to `SetContentView()`.

```
SetContentView (Resource.Layout.POIDetail);

_nameEditText = FindViewById<EditText> (Resource.Id.nameEditText);
_descrEditText = FindViewById<EditText> (
  Resource.Id.descrEditText);
_addrEditText = FindViewById<EditText> (Resource.Id.addrEditText);
_latEditText = FindViewById<EditText> (Resource.Id.latEditText);
_longEditText = FindViewById<EditText> (Resource.Id.longEditText);
_poiImageView = FindViewById<ImageView>
  (Resource.Id.poiImageView);
```

Adding navigation to POIDetailActivity

There are two scenarios where we need to navigate from `POIListActivity` to `POIDetailActivity`, when we select **New** to create a new POI or when we select an existing POI to display and update. In both of these scenarios, we need to start `POIDetailActivity`. The main difference between the two scenarios is that when selecting an existing POI to update, we will have an ID to pass to the detail View; when creating a new POI, we will not.

Navigating on new action

We'll start with the simplest scenario first. The `Activity` class provides a method named `StartActivity()`, which can be used in a number of different scenarios. In our simple scenario, we are using it in its most basic form. All that we need to do is to invoke `StartActivity()` passing in a type for the activity we want to start. The following listing demonstrates the code that needs to be added in the placeholder we added to `POIListActivity` within the `OnOptionsItemSelected()` method:

```
case Resource.Id.actionNew:
StartActivity (typeof(POIDetailActivity));
return true;
```

Navigating on POI Click

In the second scenario, we need to pass the ID for the clicked POI to display `POIDetailActivity`. To accomplish this we will use the `Intent` class. The `Intent` class can be used in conjunction with `StartActivity()` in order to launch various types of activities. We will use the `Intent` class to launch `POIDetailActivity` and pass the ID of the selected POI.

First, we need to construct an instance of `Intent` by providing the current activity for context and the type of activity that will receive the intent; in our case, `POIDetailActivity`. The following listing demonstrates how to properly construct the intent.

```
Intent poiDetailIntent =new Intent (this,
   typeof(POIDetailActivity));
```

The `Intent` object has an `Extras` property that acts as a bundle for addition, or extra data that you would like to send to a receiving activity. The `Intent` class provides a series of overloaded versions of the `PutExtra()` method, which allows you to add various types of name/value pairs to the `Extras` property.

```
poiDetailIntent.PutExtra ("poiId", poi.Id);
```

The last step is a call to `StartActivity()`, passing in the Intent we constructed.

```
StartActivity (poiDetailIntent);
```

The next stop will be the `OnCreate()` method of `POIDetailActivity`.

Receiving data in POIDetailActivity

When we get to the `OnCreate()` method of the `POIDetail` View, we need access to the POI ID so that we can retrieve and display it. Each activity has an `Intent` property that contains the intent and corresponding information that was used to start it. The `Intent` class provides a number of methods for accessing any of the `Extras` setup for the intent. To start with we would like to know if an extra was set up with the name `poiId`. We can determine this by calling `HasExtra ("poiId")`; if `false` is returned, we can assume that we are creating a new POI; otherwise, we need to retrieve the value of the extra. The `Intent` class has a series of `GetXXExtra()` methods where `XX` represents the type for the value of a name/value pair. In our case we can use the `GetIntExtra()` method on the intent to get the ID passed in from `POIListActivity`. The `GetIntExtra()` method accepts a string (which is the name for the name/value pair originally set on the intent) and an integer (which specifies a default to return if a value was not specified for the name passed in). The following listing shows what is needed in the `OnCreate()` method of `POIDetailActivity`:

```
// Private declarations
PointOfInterest _poi;

if (Intent.HasExtra ("poiId")) {
int poiId = Intent.GetIntExtra ("poiId", -1);
   _poi = POIData.Service.GetPOI (poiId);
}
```

```
else
  _poi = new PointOfInterest ();
```

Populating user interface widgets

At this point we have a reference to POI, but we have not taken any action to populate the content of our user interface widgets. This is pretty straightforward. EditText has a property named Text, which we can set to initialize the content for the widget. Create a simple method named UpdateUI(), which performs the task of moving the content to the user interface widgets; call this method at the end of the OnCreate() method. The following listing shows what is needed for UpdateUI():

```
protected void UpdateUI()
{
  _nameEditText.Text = _poi.Name;
  _descrEditText.Text = _poi.Description;
  _addrEditText.Text = _poi.Address;
  _latEditText.Text = _poi.Latitude.ToString ();
  _longEditText.Text = _poi.Longitude.ToString ();

}
```

You should be able to run POIApp now and test the navigation and viewing of data.

Adding Save and Delete actions

Using POIDetailActivity, users can choose to save new or existing POIs, or delete existing POIs. We need a way to accomplish these tasks from the user interface. We will use ActionBar again and add two actions, Save and Delete.

The following listing shows what is needed for POIDetailMenu.xml:

```
<menu xmlns:android="http://schemas.android.com/apk/res/android">
<item android:id="@+id/actionSave"
  android:icon="@drawable/ic_save"
  android:title="Save"
  android:showAsAction="ifRoom" />
<item android:id="@+id/actionDelete"
  android:icon="@drawable/ic_delete"
  android:title="Delete"
  android:showAsAction="ifRoom" />
</menu>
```

Note that each menu item has an icon specified. These icons can be found in the [assets location]\drawable folder.

The OnCreateOptionsMenu() and OnOptionsItemSelected() methods are also very similar to what we created in the previous chapter. The following code snippet is the modified version:

```
public override bool OnCreateOptionsMenu(IMenu menu)
{
MenuInflater.Inflate(Resource.Menu.POIDetailMenu, menu);
   return base.OnCreateOptionsMenu(menu);
}

public override bool OnOptionsItemSelected (IMenuItem item)
{
  switch (item.ItemId)
  {
    case Resource.Id.actionSave:
    SavePOI ();
    return true;

    case Resource.Id.actionDelete:
    DeletePOI ();
    return true;

    default :
    return base.OnOptionsItemSelected(item);
  }
}
```

In this case notice that we have added the methods SavePOI() and DeletePOI(), which get called to do all the work. This keeps the OnOptionsItemSelected() method clean and concise.

Disabling the Delete action

One thing that's different in POIDetailView is that we have a scenario where we need to disable an action. If a new POI is being created, the Delete action should not be allowed. We get a chance to make these types of changes in the OnPrepareOptionsMenu() method.

The following listing shows how to disable the Delete action when a new
POI is being entered:

```
public override bool OnPrepareOptionsMenu (IMenu menu)
{
  base.OnPrepareOptionsMenu (menu);

  // disable delete for a new POI
  if (!_poi.Id.HasValue) {
      IMenuItem item =
      menu.FindItem (Resource.Id.actionDelete);
    item.SetEnabled (false);
  }

  return true;
}
```

Notice that IMenu provides a FindItem() method that can be used to obtain
a reference to a specific IMenuItem, which in turn provides the SetEnabled()
method for enabling and disabling actions.

Creating SavePOI()

The SavePOI() method was created so that we could avoid placing a lot of logic
in the OnOptionsItemSelected() method. The SavePOI() methods needs to
accomplish the following:

1. Validate the user input.
2. Move data from the user interface widgets to the POI entity properties.
3. Call SavePOI() on POIJsonService.
4. Close the POIDetailActivity activity by calling Finish().

We will cover validation in an upcoming section and focus now on the remaining
three items. The following listing shows what should be present in SavePOI():

```
protected void SavePOI()
{
  _poi.Name = _nameEditText.Text;
  _poi.Description = _descrEditText.Text;
  _poi.Address = _addrEditText.Text;
```

```
_poi.Latitude = Double.Parse (_latEditText.Text);
_poi.Longitude = Double.Parse (_longEditText.Text);

POIData.Service.SavePOI (_poi);
Finish ();
}
```

Creating DeletePOI()

Like `SavePOI()`, the `DeletePOI()` method was created to simplify the logic in
`OnOptionsItemSelected()`. The `DeletePOI()` method needs to accomplish
the following:

1. Call `DeletePOI()` on `POIJsonService`.
2. Close the `POIDetailActivity` activity by calling `Finish()`.

The following listing shows what should be present in the `DeletePOI()` method:

```
protected void DeletePOI()
{
  POIData.Service.DeletePOI (_poi);
  Finish ();
}
```

You should now be able to run the app and add, change, and delete POIs.

Adding validation

Any nontrivial app will have some level of the validation required. The `POIApp` app
is somewhat trivial, but we have a small set of rules we need to enforce that will
facilitate the discussion.

Property	Rule
Name	Cannot be empty or null.
Latitude	Valid decimal number between `-90` and `90`.
Longitude	Valid decimal number between `-180` and `180`.

Using the EditText.Error property

The EditText widget has a string property named Error, which simplifies the effort of displaying errors to the user, particularly if you want to be able to show all the fields with errors at once. The following screenshot displays the error received for leaving the **Name** field empty:

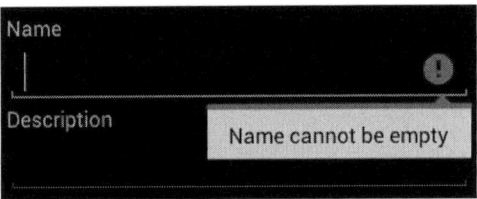

To use this facility, simply set the property to an error message and clear the property when no errors exist. The following example demonstrates implementing the rule for the **Name** property.

```
bool errors = false;

if (String.IsNullOrEmpty (_nameEditText.Text)) {
_nameEditText.Error = "Name cannot be empty";
  errors = true;
}
else
   _nameEditText.Error = null;
```

Notice the local Boolean variable named errors, which is used to keep track of whether any errors have been found. Edits for Latitude and Longitude are a little more involved, as you need to account for converting text to a double value and allow for a null value to be specified. The following code demonstrates one of the approaches to implement the edits:

```
double? tempLatitude = null;
if (!String.IsNullOrEmpty(_latEditText.Text)) {
  try {
    tempLatitude = Double.Parse(_latEditText.Text);
    if ((tempLatitude > 90) | (tempLatitude < -90)) {
      _latEditText.Error = "Latitude must be a decimal value
        between -90 and 90";
      errors = true;
    }
    else
       _latEditText.Error = null;
  }
```

```
catch {
  _latEditText.Error = "Latitude must be valid decimal number";
errors = true;
}
}
```

Implement the rules identified at the start of this section in the `SavePOI()` method using the `EditText.Error` property.

The actual updating of the POI properties and saving should only be performed if all of the edits are passed. The following listing shows one of the ways to structure the logic:

```
if (!errors) {
  _poi.Name = _nameEditText.Text;
  _poi.Description = _descrEditText.Text;
  _poi.Address = _addrEditText.Text;
  _poi.Latitude = tempLatitude;
  _poi.Longitude = tempLongitude;
  POIData.Service.SavePOI (_poi);
  Finish ();
}
```

Notice that the `Finish()` method is called at the end of the preceding code snippet. This causes the `POIDetailActivity` activity to be closed and the previous activity on the stack will be brought back to the foreground; in our case, `POIListActivity`. Refer to the code bundle for a more complete example.

Run `POIApp` and confirm that the validations are working correctly.

Adding a Delete confirmation prompt

It's best practice for apps to provide a confirmation before performing any type of destructive update, particularly if it cannot be undone. As such we need to provide a confirmation for the `Delete` action. Fortunately, Android makes this relatively easy with the `AlertDialog` and `AlertDialog.Builder` classes. The `AlertDialog` class allows you to display a modal confirmation dialog. The `AlertDialog.Builder` class is an embedded class that helps to construct an instance of an `AlertDialog` method; you can think of it as a factory class. The steps are as follows:

1. Create an instance of `AlertDialog.Builder`.

2. Set various properties on the builder instance, such as the message, the button text, the calling of event handlers when a button is clicked, and so on.

3. Call `Show()` on the instance of `AlertDialog.Builder` to create and display an instance of `AlertDialog`.

   In our case we want an `AlertDialog` class with a simple message and an **OK** and **Cancel** button. When **Cancel** is clicked on, we simply need to close the dialog and not do anything else. When **OK** is clicked on, we need to delete the POI and close the activity.

4. Create an event handler that will be called when **OK** is clicked on and move the `delete` and `finish` logic into this new event handler. The following listing depicts these changes:

```
protected void ConfirmDelete(object sender, EventArgs e)
{
  POIData.Service.DeletePOI (_poi);
  Finish ();
}
```

5. Add the logic that constructs the `AlertDialog` class into the existing `DeletePOI()` method. The following listing depicts this logic:

```
protected void DeletePOI()
{
  AlertDialog.Builder alertConfirm =
          new AlertDialog.Builder(this);
  alertConfirm.SetCancelable(false);
  alertConfirm.SetPositiveButton("OK", ConfirmDelete);
  alertConfirm.SetNegativeButton("Cancel", delegate {});
  alertConfirm.SetMessage(String.Format("Are you sure you
    want to delete {0}?", _poi.Name));
  alertConfirm.Show();
}
```

The `SetPositiveButton()` and `SetNegativeButton()` methods allow button captions and event handlers to be specified. In the case of the NEGATIVE button **Cancel**, we provide an empty event handler because there is nothing to do; Android will take care of closing the dialog. `AlertDialog` also provides a NEUTRAL button.

 On devices prior to Honeycomb, the button order (left to right) was POSITIVE - NEUTRAL - NEGATIVE. On newer devices using the Holo theme, the button order (left to right) is NEGATIVE - NEUTRAL - POSITIVE.

Run POIApp and verify if the delete confirmation is working correctly.

Toasting success

Sometimes it is nice to have a positive confirmation when actions are completed successfully. Toasts are a way within Android to display a short message that will disappear after a specified amount of time. The `Toast` class is used to accomplish this. The following listing depicts calls to `MakeText()` and `Show()`:

```
Toast toast = Toast.MakeText (this, String.Format ("{0} deleted.",
   _poi.Name), ToastLength.Short);
toast.Show();
```

Add toasts prior to the call to `Finish()` in both the `SavePOI()` and `ConfirmDelete()` methods. Refer to the source in the code bundle for an example.

Run `POIApp` and confirm that the toasts are displaying correctly.

Refreshing POIListActivity

Actions we take on `POIDetailActivity`, such as `Save` and `Delete`, have an effect on the data that would have been previously displayed on `POIListActivity`; we need to be sure that `ListView` on `POIListActivity` is refreshed when it becomes active again. `BaseAdapter<>` provides a method `NotifyDataSetChanged()`, which can be used to cause an adapter to refresh or repopulate an adapter View. The best place to call `NotifyDataSetChange()` would be in the `OnResume()` method. As you may recall from *Chapter 1, The Anatomy of an Android App*, when an activity is moved to the background due to the start of a new activity, the `OnPause()` method is called. This would have happened for `POIListActivity` when `POIDetailActivity` was started. When `POIDetailActivity` is completed, `POIListActivity` will be brought back to the foreground and the `OnResume()` method will be called. The following listing shows what is needed to refresh `POIListActivity`:

```
protected override void OnResume (){
  base.OnResume ();

  _adapter.NotifyDataSetChanged ();
}
```

Wrapping up

We have covered a lot of ground in this chapter. The following screenshot shows what the detailed View should look like. If you have any unintended deviations, you can refer to the code bundle:

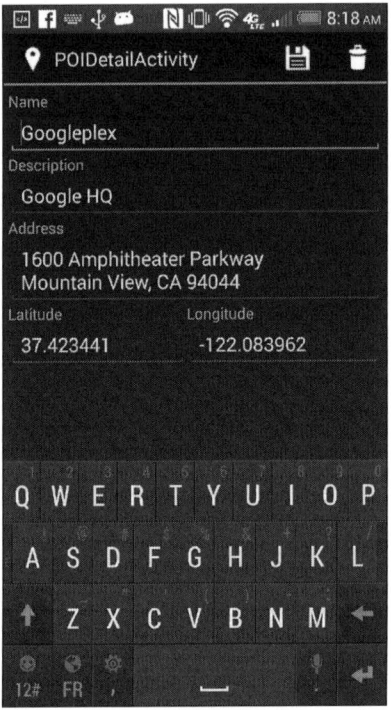

Screenshots can be captured from within the **Android Device Monitor** (**ADM**). Simply start ADM, select an emulator or connected device from the list, and click on the **Screen Capture** button just above the list.

Summary

In this chapter we developed a detailed View which allows for the viewing, updating, and deleting of POIs, as well as the navigation between the POIListActivity and POIDetailActivity. In the next chapter, we will integrate our app with Android's location services.

7

Making POIApp Location Aware

One of the most interesting aspects for mobile development is interacting with device capabilities such as motion sensors, cameras, and location sensors. While these capabilities are new and fun to many developers, they can also bring a great deal of value to the users of our mobile apps. In this chapter, we will walk through adding location awareness to POIApp including the following topics:

- Setting application permissions
- Obtaining the current longitude and latitude
- Obtaining the address for a longitude and latitude
- Calculating the distance between two locations
- Displaying a POI within the map app

Location services

While working with location services on the Android platform, you will primarily work with an instance of LocationManager. The process is fairly straightforward as follows:

1. Obtain a reference to an instance of LocationManager.
2. Use the instance of LocationManager to request location change notifications, either ongoing or a single notification.
3. Process OnLocationChange() callbacks.

Android devices generally provide two different means for determining a location: GPS and Network. When requesting location change notifications, you must specify the provider you wish to receive updates from. The Android platform defines a set of string constants for the following providers:

Provider Name	Description
GPS_PROVIDER (gps)	This provider determines a location using satellites. Depending on conditions, this provider may take a while to return a location fix. This requires the ACCESS_FINE_LOCATION permission.
NETWORK_PROVIDER (network)	This provider determines a location based on the availability of a cell tower and Wi-Fi access points. Its results are retrieved by means of a network lookup.
PASSIVE_PROVIDER (passive)	This provider can be used to passively receive location updates when other applications or services request them without actually having to request for the locations yourself. It requires the ACCESS_FINE_ LOCATION permission, although if the GPS is not enabled, this provider might only return coarse fixes.

You will notice specific permissions in the provider descriptions that must be set on an app to be used.

Setting app permissions

App permissions are specified in the AndroidManifest.xml file. To set the appropriate permissions, perform the following steps:

1. Double-click on Properties/AndroidManifest.xml in the **Solution** pad. The file will be opened in the manifest editor. There are two tabs at the bottom of the screen, **Application** and **Source**, which can be used to toggle between viewing a form for editing the file or the raw XML as follows:

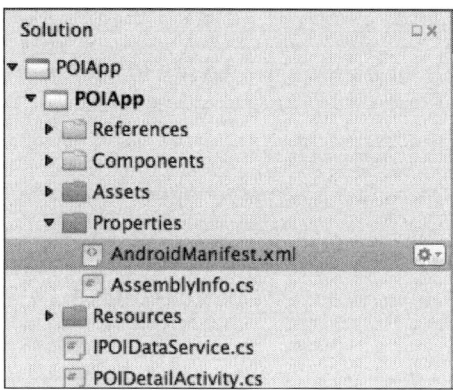

2. In the **Required permissions** list, check **AccessCoarseLocation**, **AccessFineLocation**, and **Internet**. Select **File | Save**.

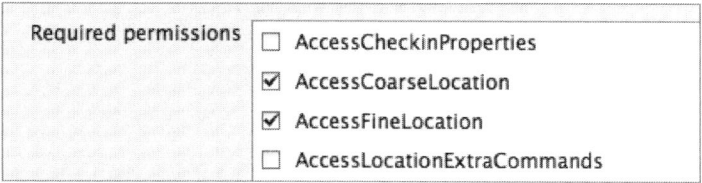

3. Switch to the Source View to view the XML as follows:

```
1 <?xml version="1.0" encoding="utf-8"?>
2 <manifest xmlns:android="http://schemas.android.com/apk/res/android" android:versi
3     <uses-sdk />
4     <application android:label="POIApp"></application>
5     <uses-permission android:name="android.permission.ACCESS_FINE_LOCATION" />
6     <uses-permission android:name="android.permission.ACCESS_COARSE_LOCATION" />
7     <uses-permission android:name="android.permission.INTERNET" />
8 </manifest>
```

Configuring the emulator

To use an emulator for development, this chapter will require the emulator to be configured with Google APIs so that the address lookup and navigation to map app works.

To install and configure Google APIs, perform the following steps:

1. From the main menu, select **Tools | Open Android SDK Manager**.

2. Select the platform version you are using, check **Google APIs**, and click on **Install 1 package...**, as seen in the following screenshot:

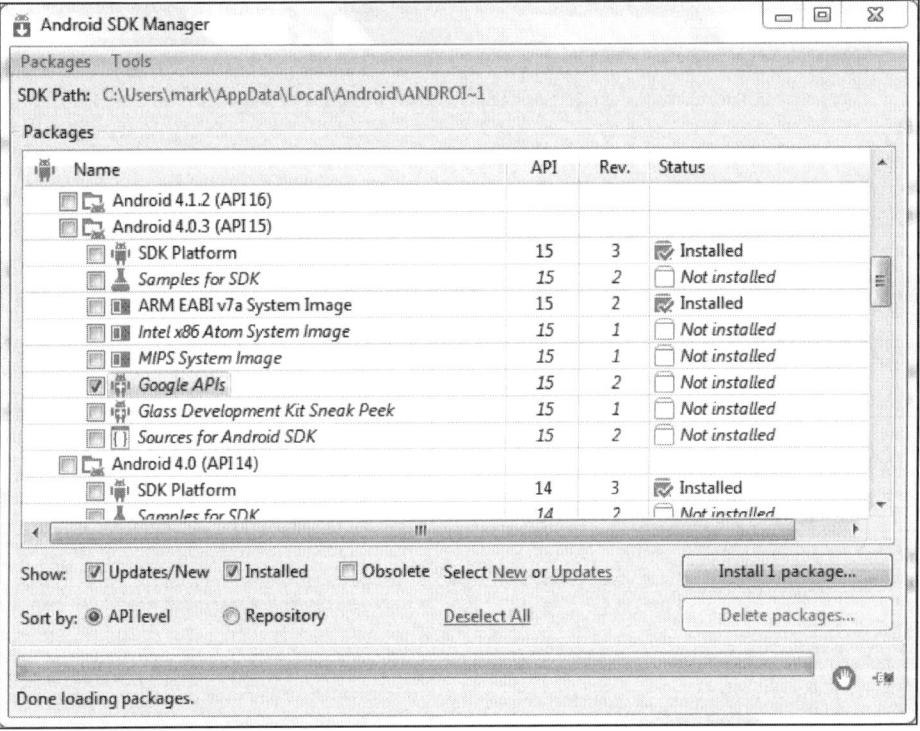

3. After the installation is complete, close the **Android SDK Manager** and from the main menu, select **Tools | Open Android Emulator Manager**.

4. Select the emulator you want to configure and click on **Edit**.

5. For **Target**, select the Google APIs entry for the API level you want to work with; for example, **Google APIs (Google Inc.) – API Level 15** was used for the development of the book examples as follows:

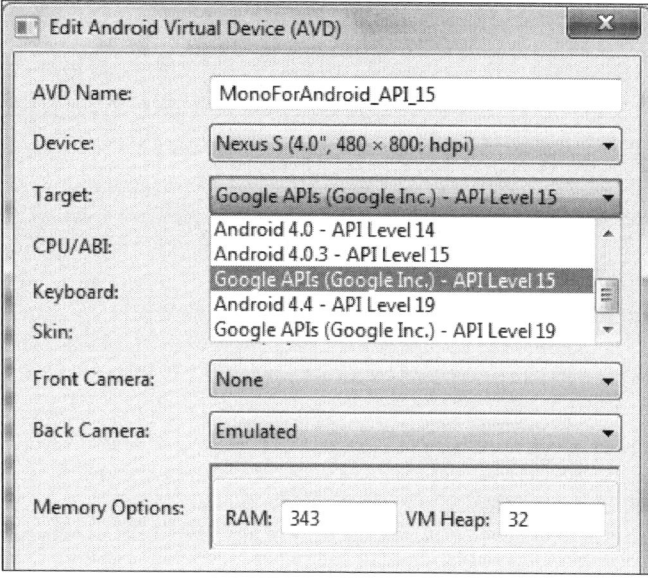

6. Click on **OK** to save.

Obtaining an instance of LocationManager

The LocationManager class is a system service that provides access to the location and bearing of a device, if the device supports these services. You do not explicitly create an instance of LocationManager; instead, you request an instance from a Context object using the GetSystemService() method. In most cases, the Context object is a subtype of Activity. The following code depicts declaring a reference of a LocationManager class and requesting an instance:

```
LocationManager _locMgr;
. . .
_locMgr = GetSystemService (Context.LocationService) as
  LocationManager;
```

Requesting location change notifications

The LocationManager class provides a series of overloaded methods that can be used to request location update notifications. If you simply need a single update, you can call RequestSingleUpdate(); to receive ongoing updates, call RequestLocationUpdate().

Prior to requesting location updates, you must identify the location provider that should be used. In our case, we simply want to use the most accurate provider available at the time. This can be accomplished by specifying the criteria for the desired provider using an instance of `Android.Location.Criteria`. The following code example shows how to specify the minimum criteria:

```
Criteria criteria = new Criteria();
criteria.Accuracy = Accuracy.NoRequirement;
criteria.PowerRequirement = Power.NoRequirement;
```

Now that we have the criteria, we are ready to request updates as follows:

```
_locMgr.RequestSingleUpdate (criteria, this, null);
```

Implementing ILocationListener

You will notice that the second parameter to `RequestSingleUpdate()` must be an object that implements `ILocationListener`, which defines the following methods:

- `void OnLocationChanged (Location location);`
- `void OnProviderDisabled (string provider);`
- `void OnProviderEnabled (string provider);`
- `void OnStatusChanged (string provider, Availability status, Bundle extras);`

For the most part, we will create blank stubs for all of the methods except `OnLocationChanged()`. While writing more sophisticated applications, it will be useful to provide implementations for some of the other methods. For example, you might call `RequestLocationUpdate()` to begin receiving updates and then receive a notification via `OnProviderEnabled()` that a preferred provider is now available, in which case you would want to stop updates and start them again using the preferred provider.

Adding location services to POIApp

In POIApp, we have the following two different scenarios for requesting location updates:

- On the `POIListActivity` class, we need to calculate the distance to each listed POI. In this scenario, we want to request location change notifications on an ongoing basis and use the most current location to calculate the distance.
- On `POIDetailActivity`, we would like to request the current location when adding a new POI. In this scenario, we will want to request a single location change notification.

Adding location services to POIListActivity

Now that we have some idea of how to add location services to an app, let's add location services to POIListActivity as follows:

1. Declare a private instance of LocationManager and obtain a reference in OnCreate() as follows:

```
LocationManager _locMgr;

. . .

protected override void OnCreate (Bundle bundle)
{
  base.OnCreate (bundle);
  SetContentView (Resource.Layout.POIList);

  _locMgr = GetSystemService (Context.LocationService) as
    LocationManager;

. . .
```

2. In OnResume(), obtain the best location provider and call RequestLocationUpdates() to start receiving updates as follows:

```
protected override void OnResume ()
{
  base.OnResume ();

  _adapter.NotifyDataSetChanged ();

  Criteria criteria = new Criteria ();
  criteria.Accuracy = Accuracy.NoRequirement;
  criteria.PowerRequirement = Power.NoRequirement;

  string provider = _locMgr.GetBestProvider (criteria,
    true);
  _locMgr.RequestLocationUpdates(provider, 20000, 100,
    this);
}
```

3. Add a call to RemoveUpdates() in OnPause(). This eliminates unnecessary processing of location changes when the POIListActivity class is not visible, as shown in the following code:

```
protected override void OnPause ()
{
  base.OnPause ();
  _locMgr.RemoveUpdates (this);
}
```

4. Specify that `POIListActivity` implements `Android.Locations.ILocationListener` and implement stub methods using the `Refactor|Implement` interface. Remove any code placed in the stub methods, we will provide logic for `OnLocationChange()`.

5. Add a `CurrentLocation` property to `POIListViewAdapter`. The `POIListActivity` class will use this property to communicate location changes to the adapter:

```
public Location CurrentLocation { get; set; }
```

6. Add a logic in `OnLocationChanged()` to set `CurrentLocation` on `POIListViewAdapter` when a location change is received and call `NotifyDataSetChange()` to cause the `ListView` to be refreshed as follows:

```
public void OnLocationChanged (Location location)
{
  _adapter.CurrentLocation = location;
  _adapter.NotifyDataSetChanged ();
}
```

7. Add logic to the `GetView()` method on `POIListViewAdapter` to calculate the distance between the `CurrentLocation` and a POI's location properties and update `distanceTextView` with the results. The calculation should only be done if `CurrentLocation` is not `null` and the `Latitude` and `Longitude` properties for the POI being added to the `ListView` are not `null`. If any of these values are `null`, simply place `??` in the distance field to indicate it cannot be calculated at this time as follows:

```
if ((CurrentLocation != null) && (poi.Latitude.HasValue) &&
  (poi.Longitude.HasValue)) {
  Location poiLocation = new Location ("");
  poiLocation.Latitude = poi.Latitude.Value;
  poiLocation.Longitude = poi.Longitude.Value;
  float distance = CurrentLocation.DistanceTo (poiLocation)
    * 0.000621371F;
  view.FindViewById<TextView>
  (Resource.Id.distanceTextView).Text = String.Format
    ("{0:0,0.00} miles", distance);
}
else {
  view.FindViewById<TextView>
    (Resource.Id.distanceTextView).Text = "??";
}
```

Now, run `POIApp` and view the results in `POIListView`.

Adding location services to POIDetailActivity

The steps for adding location services to POIDetailActivity will be very similar to the previous section, but will be slightly simpler.

Updating the user interface

Prior to adding the logic, we need to add a few buttons to our app; one for getting our location and one for navigating to the map, which we will cover later in this chapter. We can add these as a row of buttons at the bottom of POIDetail.axml, as depicted in the following screenshot:

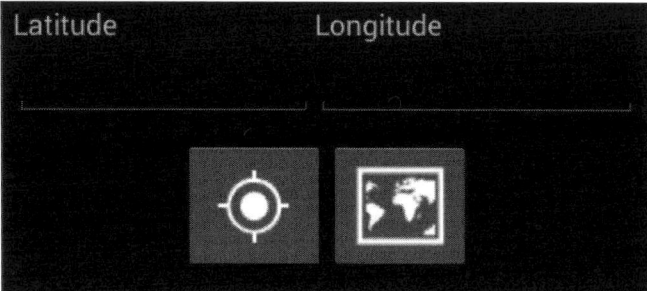

Using ImageButton allows a drawable class to be specified.

To add the ImageButton widgets, perform the following steps:

1. Add a LinearLayout instance to the bottom of POIDetail.axml just below the TableLayout used to arrange the latitude and longitude content. The orientation should be "horizontal".

2. On the LinearLayout instance, the orientation should be horizontal, the content should be wrapped (both height and width), and it should be centered horizontally in the parent. The layout gravity can be used to center content horizontally within its parent. The top and bottom padding of 10dp will provide a good spacing for the buttons.

3. Add the two ImageButton widgets, locationImageButton and mapImageButton, within the LinearLayout instance. Images for these buttons can be found in the drawable folder in the assets location.

4. The following XML code shows the result:

    ```
    . . .
    </TableLayout>
    <LinearLayout
      p1:orientation="horizontal"
      p1:layout_width="wrap_content"
    ```

```
p1:layout_height="wrap_content"
p1:layout_gravity="center_horizontal"
p1:minWidth="25px"
p1:minHeight="25px"
p1:layout_marginTop="10dp"
p1:layout_marginBottom="10dp">
<ImageButton
  p1:src="@drawable/ic_locate"
  p1:layout_width="wrap_content"
  p1:layout_height="wrap_content"
  p1:id="@+id/locationImageButton" />
<ImageButton
  p1:src="@drawable/ic_map"
  p1:layout_width="wrap_content"
  p1:layout_height="wrap_content"
  p1:id="@+id/mapImageButton" />
</LinearLayout>
```

Adding the code

Now that we have buttons on the UI, we can add the code to obtain the location as follows:

1. Declare a private instance of LocationManager and obtain a reference in OnCreate() in the same way we did for POIListView in the previous section.

2. Add a GetLocationClicked event handler and hook it up to the ImageButton as follows:

    ```
    _locationImageButton = FindViewById<ImageButton>
      (Resource.Id.locationImageButton);

    _locationImageButton.Click += GetLocationClicked;
    ```

3. Add a call to `RequestSingleUpdate()` in `GetLocationClicked()`. The `RequestSingleUpdate()` method allows for a `Criteria` object to be passed in so that we do not need a separate call to `GetBestProvider()` as follows:

```
protected void GetLocationClicked(object sender, EventArgs   e)
{
    Criteria criteria = new Criteria();
    criteria.Accuracy = Accuracy.NoRequirement;
    criteria.PowerRequirement = Power.NoRequirement;

    _locMgr.RequestSingleUpdate (criteria, this, null);
}
```

4. Specify that `POIDetailActivity` implements `Android.Locations.ILocationListener` and implement stub methods using the `Refactor|Implement` interface. Remove any code placed in the stub methods; we will provide a logic for `OnLocationChange()`.

5. Add a logic in `OnLocationChange()` to update the location fields as follows:

```
public void OnLocationChanged (Location location)
{
    _latEditText.Text = location.Latitude.ToString();
    _longEditText.Text = location.Longitude.ToString ();
}
```

Run `POIApp` and test adding a new POI and getting the location. While running the app in the emulator, you will notice that apparently nothing happens when the **location** button is clicked. The app is actually waiting for a callback to `OnLocationChanged()` from the location manager; to trigger this callback, you must use the Android Device Monitor.

To trigger `OnLocationChanged()`, perform the following steps:

1. Start ADM and select the emulator instance on the left-hand side.

2. Click on the **Emulator Control** tab on the right-hand side. If the **Emulator Control** tab is not present, navigate to **Window | Show View** to display the tab. Notice that at the bottom of the panel, there is a nested tab titled **Location Controls**, as shown in the following screenshot:

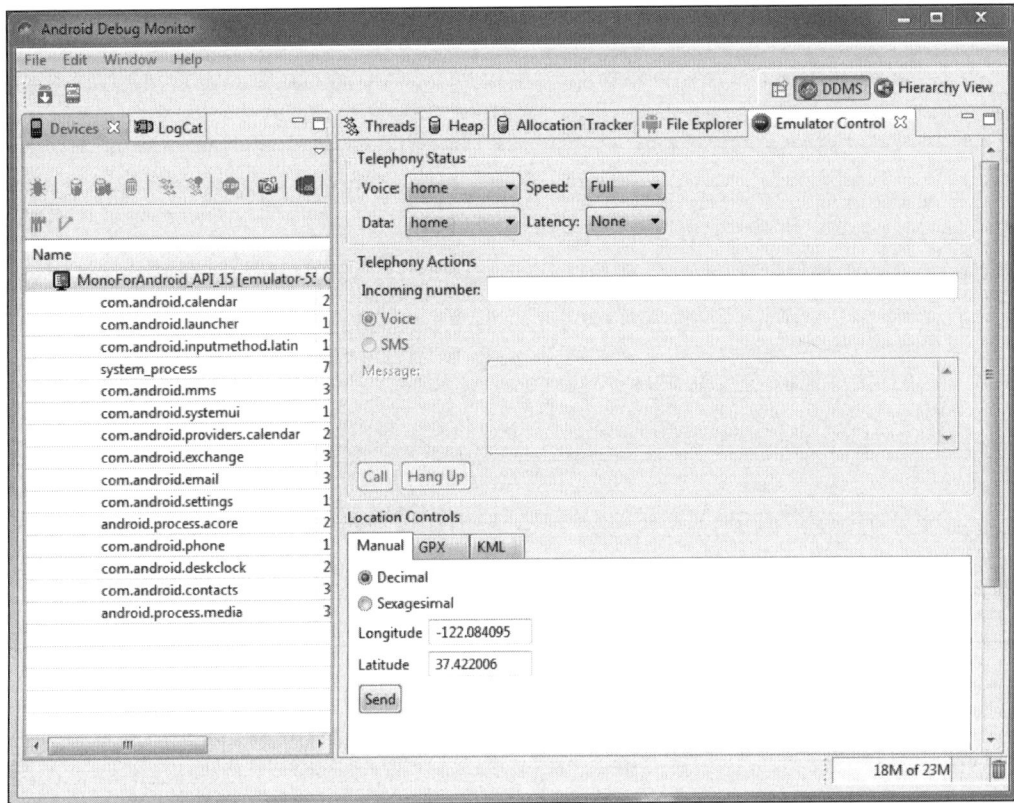

3. Select the **Manual** tab, adjust **Longitude** and **Latitude**, if desired, and click on **Send**. This will cause the OnLocationChanged() method to be fired on POIDetailActivity.

Note the other two tabs under **Location Controls**, that is **GPX** and **KML**. These tabs can be used to load a series of location updates from a file and play them back to your app to test more sophisticated scenarios.

Getting an address for a location

Another useful feature provided by the Android platform is called **Geocoding**. This is the process of obtaining the location in terms of latitude and longitude from a known address. Android also supports **Reverse Geocoding**, which is what you would expect from the name, obtaining an address from a known location.

The `Android.Locations.Geocoder` class is the class used to perform geocoding and reverse geocoding. It's a very straightforward process to use, as shown in the following steps:

1. Create an instance of `Android.Locations.Geocoder`.

2. Call `GetFromLocation()` passing in the location you would like to find the address for.

3. Process the `IList<Address>` collection returned. The collection of addresses returned from `GetFromLocation()` vary in specifics; meaning, some are specific street addresses, some specify a city, country, and so on. The first address is always the most specific, so we will automatically choose it, using the following code:

```
public void OnLocationChanged (Location location)
{
  _latEditText.Text = location.Latitude.ToString();
  _longEditText.Text = location.Longitude.ToString ();

  Geocoder geocdr = new Geocoder(this);
  IList<Address> addresses = geocdr.GetFromLocation
    (location.Latitude, location.Longitude, 5);

  if (addresses.Any()) {
    UpdateAddressFields (addresses.First ());
  }
}
```

You can see that we chose to call a method to format the address information. The `FeatureName` property may contain a title such as `Golden Gate Bridge` or `Empire State Building`. More times than not, `FeatureName` will simply contain the street number. The address contains a list of address lines, which we combine and place in `_addrEditText`, as follows:

```
protected void UpdateAddressFields(Address addr)
{
  if (String.IsNullOrEmpty(_nameEditText.Text))
    _nameEditText.Text = addr.FeatureName;

  If (String.IsNullOrEmpty(_addrEditText.Text)) {
    for (int i = 0; i < addr.MaxAddressLineIndex; i++) {
      if (!String.IsNullOrEmpty(_addrEditText.Text))
```

```
            _addrEditText.Text += System.Environment.NewLine;
            _addrEditText.Text += addr.GetAddressLine (i);
        }

    }
}
```

Now, run POIApp and test adding a new POI and getting the address for a location.

Keeping the user informed

After using the **get location** button, you will notice that requests for location information take some amount of time to process; generally a few seconds or more. It would be best to keep users informed that processing is taking place so that they don't continually click on the button. The ProgressDialog class provides just the solution needed, which is a simple means of displaying a dialog with a spinning progress widget and text description of what process is taking place.

To add a progress dialog, perform the following steps:

1. Add a private variable of type ProgressDialog to POIDetailActivity as follows:

    ```
    ProgressDialog _progressDialog;
    ```

2. At the top of GetLocationClicked(), call the static method ProgressDialog.Show() saving the result in the private variable we just created. The Show(), method accepts an activity, a title, and a message as parameters. This call causes the progress dialog to be presented to the user as follows:

    ```
    _progressDialog = ProgressDialog.Show (this, "", "Obtaining
        location...");
    ```

3. At the bottom of OnLocationChanged(), call the Cancel() method on the progress dialog causing the dialog to be closed as follows:

    ```
    _progressDialog.Cancel ();
    ```

Now, run POIApp and test the new progress dialog.

Dealing with configuration changes

In the previous section, we solved the problem of keeping the user informed while they wait for location updates, but we unknowingly created another problem. As you may recall from *Chapter 1, The Anatomy of an Android App*, we mentioned that by default Android destroys and recreates an activity when a configuration change such as a device orientation change occurs.

This is done to take advantage of a feature that Android provides, which allows you to specify different layouts to use based on device orientation. In our app, we have a single folder named `layout`, which holds all our layouts. If we wanted `POIDetail.axml` to have a different layout when the device is in landscape, we would simply create a new folder in `Resources` named `layout-land` and create our alternate layout in it using the same name, `POIDetail.axml`. When Android destroys and recreates our activity because the device was rotated to landscape, our call to `SetContentView()` would cause Android to first look in `layout-land` to see if a layout exists.

This is neat, but a fallout of this approach arises when an activity initiates any type of asynchronous processing such as requesting location updates. The problem is when a configuration change takes place and Android destroys the original activity; you no longer want asynchronous callbacks to come in for the original activity.

To observe the issue, run `POIApp`, press the **get location** button, and rotate the screen. In the emulator, press *Ctrl + F11* or *Ctrl + F12* to rotate the device. If you are in the `debug` mode, you should see an exception thrown when you try and cancel the progress dialog; this is due to the fact that Android has already removed the dialog from the `view` hierarchy when it destroyed the activity.

Android provides the following ways of dealing with this issue:

- Prevent the activity from being destroyed based on specifications made for the activity in the `AndroidManifest.xml` file

- Override virtual methods on `Activity` to save and restore the state appropriately when configuration changes occur

Saving and restoring a state

To allow for saving and restoring of a state, Android provides `OnSaveInstanceState()` and `OnRestorcInstanceState()`. The `OnSaveInstanceState()` method is called as a part of the destruction of the activity due to configuration changes and allows you to save processing a state in the `Bundle` object that is passed in. The `OnRestoreInstanceState()` method is called after `OnStart()` when an activity is being reinitialized and receives the same `Bundle` object that `OnSaveInstanceState()` would have populated.

In our case, we simply want to cancel any pending location changes within `OnSaveInsatnceState()` and restart the process in `OnRestoreInstanceState()`, if we were indeed waiting for location updates when the configuration change occurred. Unfortunately, many asynchronous scenarios are far more complex than ours and are beyond what can be considered here.

To save and restore a state, perform the following steps:

1. Create a private `bool` that will be used to indicate if we are waiting for location updates as follows:

```
bool _obtainingLocation = false;
```

2. Add a line of code at the top of `GetLocationClicked()` to set this variable to `true`, and at the bottom of `OnLocationChanged()` to set this variable to `false`.

3. Override `OnSaveInstanceState()` and save the value of the processing variable and cancel any location updates that might be pending as follows:

```
protected override void OnSaveInstanceState (Bundle
  outState)
{
  base.OnSaveInstanceState (outState);

  outState.PutBoolean("obtaininglocation",
    _obtainingLocation);

  // if we were waiting on location updates; cancel
  if (_obtainingLocation) {
    _locMgr.RemoveUpdates (this);
  }
}
```

4. Override `OnRestoreInstanceState()` and restore the value of the processing variable, and if the value is `true`, restart the request for location update as follows:

```
protected override void OnRestoreInstanceState (Bundle
  savedInstanceState)
{
  base.OnRestoreInstanceState (savedInstanceState);

  _obtainingLocation =
    savedInstanceState.GetBoolean("obtaininglocation");

  // if we were waiting on location updates; restart
  if (_obtainingLocation)
    GetLocationClicked (this, new EventArgs ());
}
```

Now, run POIApp and test the changes.

Preventing activity destruction

By now, you may be wondering if we have a similar problem in POIListActivity. But we do not because of our decision to turn on and off location updates in the OnResume() and OnPause() methods. These methods are called as part of the normal construction and destruction processes. As a result, there are no scenarios where an asynchronous callback will be called after the activity is destroyed. You will, however, notice that when you change the orientation of the device, the distance labels are changed to ?? due to the activity being reconstructed. This actually provides a good opportunity to demonstrate an alternate way of dealing with this issue; preventing the activity from being destroyed. Android allows for the specification of the configChanges attribute in the activity element of the AndroidManifest.xml file. Specifying configChanges tells Android that you will take care of reconfiguring the layout, if needed, and the activity class will not be destroyed. The following code example shows how to specify that orientation and the screen size changes for POIListActivity will be dealt manually by the app:

```
<activity
  android:name="poiapp.POIListActivity"
    android:configChanges="orientation|screenSize"
      android:label="POIs" >
. . .
</activity>
```

Xamarin.Android provides a more convenient way to specify how to prevent activity destruction using an attribute on the activity class. The following code example shows the use of the ConfigurationChanges attribute;

```
[Activity (Label = "POIs", MainLauncher = true,
  ConfigurationChanges =
    (Android.Content.PM.ConfigChanges.Orientation |
      Android.Content.PM.ConfigChanges.ScreenSize))]
public class POIListActivity : Activity, ILocationListener
{
  . . .
```

After placing the ConfigurationChanges attribute on POIListActivity, run POIApp and observe that once the distances have been calculated, they will not be lost during device orientation changes.

Adding map integration

Maps are another truly cool part of mobile computing. They provide a means of navigation, finding points of interest in an area, as well as supporting many other useful scenarios.

There are two basic approaches to interfacing with maps from an app:

- Navigate to the existing Android map app showing a point of interest.
- Integrate with the Google Maps API.

The first option is much easier to implement, whereas the second option allows for tighter integration and control of the maps at the cost of more code and complexity.

We chose to go with the first option for the POIApp example for the following reasons:

- The second option requires very specific versions of Xamarin.Android binding libraries corresponding to Google Play libraries, which at the time of the writing of this book were difficult to locate and configure
- It is very difficult to get the second option working inside an emulator, meaning you would have to test and view the results of the code on an actual device, which may not be an option for all readers
- We would need to dedicate more time than we have available in this chapter to get the second option up and running

Xamarin's website contains articles with all the details required to get the second option working.

Navigating to the map app

To navigate to the map app, we will rely on the Intent class we used earlier in the book; however, rather than specifying the Activity class we want to start, we will specify the type of information we would like to view using a URI. Android contains a registry of apps that can display different types of information and will launch the most appropriate app.

The Android platform defines a set of Intent classes that can be used to launch Google apps on Android devices. The following table summarizes the Intent classes related to locations:

URI	Action
`geo:latitude,longitude`	This action opens the map application centered at a latitude or longitude.
`geo:latitude,longitude?z=zoom`	This action opens the map application centered at a latitude or longitude and zoomed to the specified level.
`geo:0,0?q=my+street+address`	This action opens the map application to the location of a street address.
`geo:0,0?q=business+near+city`	This action opens the map application and displays the annotated search results.

In our case, we have a street address, latitude and longitude, or both. If the street address is present, we should build the Intent class with it, because this will cause the street address to appear in the map app, making it more user friendly. If the street address is not present, we will build the Intent class using latitude and longitude. The following code shows the logic for building the Intent class:

```
Android.Net.Uri geoUri;
if (String.IsNullOrEmpty (_addrEditText.Text)) {
  geoUri = Android.Net.Uri.Parse (String.Format("geo:{0},{1}",
    _poi.Latitude, _poi.Longitude));
}
else {
  geoUri = Android.Net.Uri.Parse (String.Format("geo:0,0?q={0}",
    _addrEditText.Text));
}

Intent mapIntent = new Intent (Intent.ActionView, geoUri);
```

Prior to launching the Intent class, we need to be sure there is an app that can handle the Intent class; otherwise, we might end up with an unhandled exception from StartActivity().

Checking for registered map apps

Apps provide information about any capabilities they provide (the Intent classes) in their manifest files as an <intent-filter/> element. Since we are relying on an external map app to display our location for us, we should check to be sure such an app exists on the device we are running on. We accomplish this with a few calls to the PackageManager class. The PackageManager class allows you to retrieve various types of information about the application packages installed on a device. The QueryIntentActivities() method allows you to check if there are any apps available to handle a specific Intent class. The following code demonstrates the use of QueryIntentActivities():

```
PackageManager packageManager = PackageManager;
IList<ResolveInfo> activities =
  packageManager.QueryIntentActivities(mapIntent, 0);

if (activities.Count == 0) {
  AlertDialog.Builder alertConfirm = new AlertDialog.Builder
    (this);
  alertConfirm.SetCancelable (false);
  alertConfirm.SetPositiveButton ("OK", delegate {});
```

```
    alertConfirm.SetMessage ("No map app available.");
    alertConfirm.Show ();

}
else
    StartActivity (mapIntent);
```

Create a `MapClicked()` event handler, attach it to the `mapImageButton`, and fill in the logic for building and starting the `Intent` class.

Run `POIApp` and test navigating to the map from POI. You will notice that once the map app has been presented with the POI location, you have the option of choosing to navigate to it from your current location.

Summary

In this chapter, we stepped through integrating `POIApp` with location services and the Google map app. In the next chapter, we will continue integrating with device capabilities by adding integration with the camera.

8
Adding Camera App Integration

Another exciting feature of mobile computing is that most devices have some type of camera that can be used to capture photos and/or videos. This chapter will walk through the steps required to add the ability to capture a picture of a POI and will include the following topics:

- Approaches to adding camera integration
- Camera permissions and features
- Capturing and displaying a photo
- Displaying a photo in the List View

Picking an integration approach

The Android platform provides two primary ways to add camera integration to your app:

- Using existing camera apps to integrate using `intent`
- Creating your own custom activity that interacts directly with the camera using the Android API

The second approach allows for a high degree of control over how the camera View is presented to the user and how the user interacts with the View. The first approach is much simpler to implement and focuses on reusing existing apps to capture the picture. We will go with the first approach as it represents a very practical way to add camera integration.

Permissions and Features

Prior to getting into the details of adding camera integration, we will discuss more about the general permissions and features related to the camera. The following table contains the various permissions that may be required. In our case, we need not specify any of these, because we are using an external camera app to capture the picture.

Permission	Description
CAMERA	If your app requests permission to use the device's camera, this is not required if you make the request through an intent
WRITE_EXTERNAL_STORAGE	If your app saves images or videos to the devices external storage (SD card)
RECORD_AUDIO	If your app records audio with video capture
ACCESS_FINE_LOCATION	If your app tags photos with GPS location information

Camera-specific features can be set up in an app's manifest file using the `<uses-feature/>` element. The following features are defined:

Feature	Description
android.hardware.camera	The application uses the device's camera. If the device supports multiple cameras, the application uses the camera that faces away from the screen.
android.hardware.camera.autofocus	*Subfeature*. The application uses the device camera's autofocus capability.
android.hardware.camera.flash	*Subfeature*. The application uses the device camera's flash.
android.hardware.camera.front	*Subfeature*. The application uses a front-facing camera on the device.
android.hardware.camera.any	The application uses at least one camera facing any direction. Use this in preference to android.hardware.camera if a back-facing camera is not required.

In our case, we will not specify any features as requirements, but at runtime, we will check to be sure an external app is available to capture a photo. This would allow anyone to install and use our app even if their device did not have a camera.

Configuring the Emulator

If using the emulator for development, you will need to configure it to have a camera. If the computer you are using has a webcam, the emulator can use it as the camera; otherwise, you can choose to have an emulated camera.

To configure the emulator for a camera, perform the following steps:

1. From the main menu navigate to **Tools | Open Android Emulator Manager**.

2. Select the emulator you have been working with and choose **Edit**.

3. In the middle of the **Edit AVD** dialog, you will see two dropdowns; one for **Front Camera** and one for **Back Camera**. Make your selections and click on **OK**.

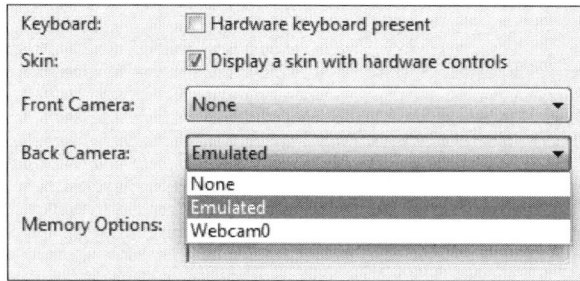

Extending the data service

Another topic we need to consider is which new features we require from the data service. Since we will be using an external camera app to capture the picture, we will have it save the picture in the same location as the JSON using a naming scheme like `poiimage<id>.jpg`. The data service will not be responsible for saving the images, but it would be convenient for it to provide a location and filename. Also, since the data service deletes POIs, it would be a good idea for it to also delete corresponding POI images, if they exist.

Defining GetImageFilename()

As we previously mentioned, the filename and location is something we should obtain from the data service. To do so, we will first add a method to the `IPOIDataService` interface and then implement it in `POIJsonServices`. The following listing shows the method we need to add to `IPOIDataService`:

```
public interface IPOIDataService
{
...
string GetImageFilename (int id);
}
```

Implementing GetImageFilename()

Now, we need to implement the method in `POIJsonService.cs`. Image files will be named as `poiimage<id>.jpg`. The following listing shows how the filename can be constructed:

```
public string GetImageFilename(int id)
{
  return Path.Combine (_storagePath, "poiimage" + id.ToString () +
    ".jpg");
}
```

Updating DeletePOI()

The `DeletePOI()` method needs to be enhanced in order to delete an image that corresponds to a POI, if one exists. The following listing shows the changes:

```
Public void DeletePOI (PointOfInterest poi)
{
  // delete POI JSON file
  if (File.Exists(GetFilename (poi.Id)))
    File.Delete (GetFilename (poi.Id));

  // delete POI image file
  if (File.Exists(GetImageFilename (poi.Id)))
    File.Delete (GetImageFilename(poi.Id));

  // remove POI from cache
  _pois.Remove (poi);
}
```

Capturing an image from POIDetailActivity

We are now ready to take on the task of capturing a photo. This will involve the following tasks:

- Adding new user interface widgets to initiate capturing a photo and display it

- Building a photo intent to navigate to an external camera app to capture a photo

- Processing the results of the photo intent and displaying a photo if one was successfully captured

The following sections describe the details of each step.

Adding UI elements

There are a few new UI elements we will need to add to support capturing an image; we need an ImageButton element to initiate the process of capturing an image, and we also need an ImageView element to display the image. We will add the new ImageButton element at the bottom of the View next to the location and map buttons. We will add the ImageView element just below the **Latitude** and **Longitude** fields and just above the buttons at the bottom. The following list shows the definition for the ImageView, which should be placed just below the TableLayout used for the **Latitude** and **Longitude** widgets:

```
    . . .
    </TableRow>
    </TableLayout>
    <ImageView
      p1:src="@android:drawable/ic_menu_gallery"
      p1:layout_width="wrap_content"
      p1:layout_height="wrap_content"
      p1:padding="10dp"
      p1:id="@+id/poiImageView"
      p1:layout_gravity="center_horizontal"
      p1:scaleType="fitCenter" />
    <LinearLayout
    . . .
```

Create a private reference object in POIDetailActivity and assign the reference in OnCreate():

```
ImageView _poiImageView;
. . .
_poiImageView = FindViewById<ImageView> (
  Resource.Id.poiImageView);
```

Now, we need a button. Start by copying the `ic_new_picture.png` icon from the `assets` folder to the project's `drawable` folder and adding it to the project in the same manner as we did in the previous chapters. Add the following button definition to the `LinearLayout` that contains the other buttons:

```
<ImageButton
  p1:src="@drawable/ic_new_picture"
  p1:layout_width="wrap_content"
  p1:layout_height="wrap_content"
  p1:id="@+id/photoImageButton" />
```

Create a private reference object in `POIDetailActivity` and assign the reference in `OnCreate()` as follows:

```
ImageButton _photoImageButton;
...
_photoImageButton =FindViewById<ImageButton> (
  Resource.Id.photoImageButton);
```

Creating the intent

To start an external camera app to capture a photo, we rely on the `Intent` class again, this time combined with an action. The following listing depicts creating an `Intent` with the image capture action:

```
Intent cameraIntent = new Intent(MediaStore.ActionImageCapture);
```

The `MediaStore.ActionImageCapture` action tells the Android platform you want to capture a photo and are willing to use any existing app that provides those capabilities.

Checking for registered camera apps

In *Chapter 7, Making POIApp Location Aware*, we used `PackageManager` to check to see if a map app was present to handle our intent. We now need to perform the same check for an app that can handle our `ActionImageCapture` intent. The following listing shows the logic we need:

```
PackageManager packageManager = PackageManager;
IList<ResolveInfo> activities =
  packageManager.QueryIntentActivities(cameraIntent, 0);
```

```
if (activities.Count == 0) {
  //display alert indicating there are no camera apps
}
else {
  //launch the cameraIntent
}
```

Providing additional information with the intent

Prior to starting the intent, we need to provide some information to the camera app that processes our request; specifically, a filename and location, and the maximum size of the resulting photo. We do this by adding Extras to the intent. The MediaStore class defines a number of standard Extras that can be added to an intent to control how an external app fulfils the intent.

Providing a filename and location

The MediaStore.ExtraOutput extra can be added to control the filename and location the external app should use in order to capture an image. We previously enhanced the data service to provide this information. Unfortunately, we will need to convert the string path we get from the data service to an instance of Android.Net.Uri, which is the expected format for camera apps that consume MediaStore.ExtraOutput.

This is a two-step process. First, we create a Java.IO.File object using the string path from the data service and then create an Android.Net.Uri object. The following listing shows how to accomplish the construction of the URI and set up the MediaStore.ExtraOutput extra:

```
Java.IO.File imageFile = new Java.IO.File(
  POIData.Service.GetImageFilename(_poi.Id.Value));

Android.Net.Uri imageUri = Android.Net.Uri.FromFile (imageFile);

cameraIntent.PutExtra (MediaStore.ExtraOutput, imageUri);
```

Providing size limit

The MediaStore.ExtraSizeLimit extra limits the image size. It is much more straightforward to set up as follows:

```
cameraIntent.PutExtra (MediaStore.ExtraSizeLimit, 1.5 * 1024);
```

Starting the intent

We are now ready to start the intent. In other cases where we used the Intent class, we were not looking for any information to be provided as a result. In this case, we are expecting the photo app to provide either a photo or a notification that the user cancelled the photo. You accomplish this by using StartActivityForResult() by passing in the intent. The StartActivityForResults() method works in conjunction with a callback to OnActivityResult(), to communicate the results of the intent. The following listing depicts the calling of StartActivityForResult():

```
const int CAPTURE_PHOTO = 0;

. . .

StartActivityForResult(cameraIntent, CAPTURE_PHOTO);
```

Notice the second parameter to StartActivityForResult(). It is an int value named requestCode that will be returned as a parameter in the callback to OnActivityResult() and help identify the original reason for launching an intent. The best practice is to define a constant value to pass in for each requestCode that can potentially cause OnActivityResult() to be called.

Completing the NewPhotoClicked() method

We have covered a number of topics related to starting the camera app in a somewhat fragmented fashion. The following listing is the complete implementation for NewPhotoClicked():

```
public void NewPhotoClicked(object sender, EventArgs e)
{
if (!_poi.Id.HasValue) {
  AlertDialog.Builder alertConfirm=new AlertDialog.Builder(this);
  alertConfirm.SetCancelable(false);
  alertConfirm.SetPositiveButton("OK", delegate {});
  alertConfirm.SetMessage(
    "You must save the POI prior to attaching a photo");
  alertConfirm.Show ();
  }
else {
    Intent cameraIntent = new Intent (
      MediaStore.ActionImageCapture);
    PackageManager packageManager = PackageManager;
    IList<ResolveInfo> activities = packageManager.
      QueryIntentActivities(cameraIntent, 0);
```

```
      if (activities.Count == 0) {
        AlertDialog.Builder alertConfirm = new
          AlertDialog.Builder(this);
        alertConfirm.SetCancelable(false);
        alertConfirm.SetPositiveButton("OK", delegate {});
        alertConfirm.SetMessage(
          "No camera app available to capture photos.");
        alertConfirm.Show ();
      }
      else {
        Java.IO.File imageFile = new Java.IO.File(
          POIData.Service.GetImageFilename(_poi.Id.Value));

        Android.Net.Uri imageUri = Android.Net.Uri.FromFile (
          imageFile);

        cameraIntent.PutExtra (MediaStore.ExtraOutput, imageUri);
        cameraIntent.PutExtra (MediaStore.ExtraSizeLimit,
          1.5 * 1024);

        StartActivityForResult (cameraIntent, CAPTURE_PHOTO);
      }
    }
  }
}
```

Processing the results of the intent

The initiating activity is notified of the results of an intent via the
OnActivityResult() callback method. The following listing shows the signature
for the OnActivityResult() method:

```
OnActivityResult (int requestCode, Result resultCode, Intent data)
```

We discussed requestCode in the previous section. The resultCode parameter
indicates the result of the intent that was launched and is of type Result,
which can have the following values:

Value	Meaning
RESULT_OK	The activity completed the request successfully.
REQUEST_CANCELED	The activity was cancelled, generally by a user action.
REQUEST_FIRST_USER	The first value that can be used for a custom meaning.

The third parameter, data, is of type Intent and can be used to pass additional information back from the activity that was launched. In our case, we are only concerned with requestCode and resultCode. The following listing shows the implementation of OnActivityResult() in POIDetailActivity:

```
protected override void OnActivityResult (int requestCode,
  Result resultCode, Intent data)
{
  if (requestCode == CAPTURE_PHOTO) {
    if (resultCode == RESULT_OK) {
    // display saved image
    Bitmap poiImage = POIData.GetImageFile (_poi.Id.Value);
    _poiImageView.SetImageBitmap (poiImage);
    if (poiImage != null)
      poiImage.Dispose ();
    }
    else {
      // let the user know the photo was cancelled
      Toast toast = Toast.MakeText (this, "No picture captured.",
        ToastLength.Short);
      toast.Show();
    }
  }
  else
    base.OnActivityResult (requestCode, resultCode, data);
}
```

Notice that when resultCode is RESULT_OK, we load the photo that was captured into a Bitmap object and then set the image for _poiImageView. This causes the image to be displayed at the bottom of the POIDetail layout. If resultCode is not RESULT_OK, we display a toast message to the user indicating that the action was cancelled.

You will also notice the magic method GetImageFile() on POIData that just showed up from nowhere. It is actually not magic; we need to add it. The GetImageFile() method is a simple utility method that accepts a POI ID and loads Android. Graphics.Bitmap using the Android utility class BitmapFactory. The following listing shows the GetImageFile() method:

```
public static Bitmap GetImageFile(int poiId)
{
  string filename = Service.GetImageFilename (poiId);
  if (File.Exists (filename)) {
```

```
        Java.IO.File imageFile = new Java.IO.File (filename);
        return BitmapFactory.DecodeFile (imageFile.Path);
    }
    else
        return null;
}
```

We could have simply embedded this code in `OnActivityResult()`, but we will need the same functionality in a few more places. We could have also chosen to add the method to `POIJsonService`, but that would have required us to introduce specific Android types to the data service, which would have limited its reuse in other platforms.

We have added a lot of code. Run `POIApp` and test adding a photo.

Displaying existing images in POIDetailActivity

You may have realized from experimenting with `POIApp` that images only show up after capturing them; if you go back to the list View and select the same POI, the previously captured image will not be displayed. To solve this, we need to add some lines of code to the `OnCreate()` method to load the image if an ID for a POI was passed in with the intent.

```
if (Intent.HasExtra ("poiId")) {
    int poiId = Intent.GetIntExtra ("poiId", -1);
    _poi = POIData.Service.GetPOI (poiId);
    Bitmap poiImage = POIData.GetImageFile (_poi.Id.Value);
    _poiImageView.SetImageBitmap (poiImage);
    if (poiImage != null)
        poiImage.Dispose ();
}
else
    _poi = new PointOfInterest ();
```

Displaying POI images in POIListActivity

The last task in completing our app is to add the logic to display POI images in `POIListActivity`. As you may recall from the previous chapters, `POIListViewAdapter` is responsible for creating and setting up the `POIListItem` layout for the POIs listed. The changes we need to make are in the `GetView()` method of `POIListViewAdapter`. The following listing shows the code that should be added:

```
//load image into image View
Bitmap poiImage = POIData.GetImageFile (poi.Id.Value);
view.FindViewById<ImageView> (
   Resource.Id.poiImageView).SetImageBitmap (poiImage);
if (poiImage != null)
   poiImage.Dispose ();
```

Run POIApp and view the results.

You have now completed an Android app that exercises many of the features you will need to utilize for developing a professional app. I hope these chapters have provided a good launchpad for you and I wish you the best of luck as you continue developing with Xamain.Android!

Summary

In this chapter, we have completed POIApp by adding integration with the camera. We now have an app that demonstrates many of the features of the Android platform and while the app is relatively simple in nature, the hope is that we have provided a broad base of information to move forward in your career, developing Android apps. In the last chapter, we will discuss the many options available for distributing Android apps and the process you go through to accomplish its distribution.

9
Deploying Your App

An app is useful if everyone can enjoy it and that means finding a way to make it available to the masses. In this chapter, we will look into the options you have for deploying your app and discuss various aspects of getting your app ready for deployment. This chapter covers the following topics:

- App distribution options
- Compiling and linking for release
- Publishing a signed APK

App distribution options

Android developers have a number of options for distributing their applications, which include the following:

- Website links
- E-mail attachments
- App stores

Website links and e-mail attachments are pretty straightforward, easy to accomplish, and may be suitable for some apps that are used primarily internally by a company or by a small group of friends or associates. Prior to installing apps from a website link or an e-mail attachment, you must first update a security setting on your device to allow apps to be installed from unknown sources. Refer the following screenshot:

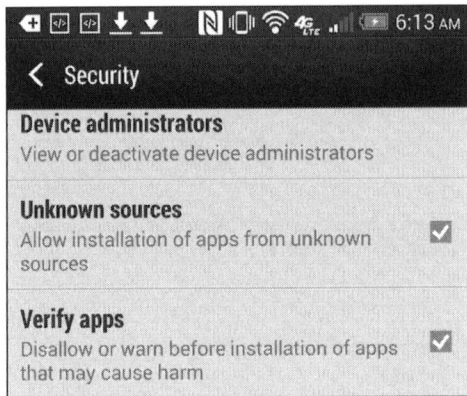

After enabling this option, you will be prompted to install an app when selecting an e-mail attachment or a web link that is an APK, as shown in the following screenshot:

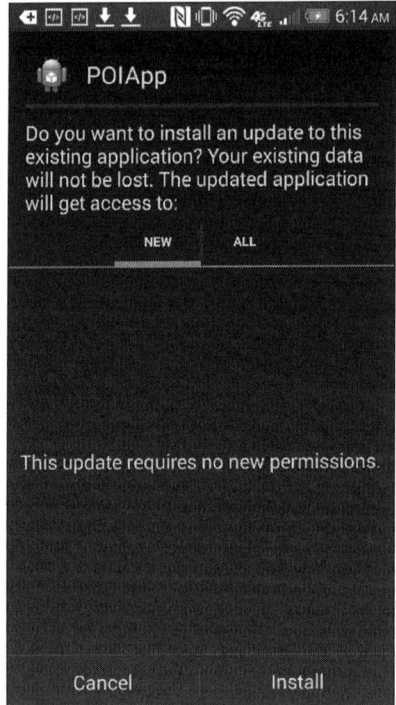

For general consumers, website links and e-mails as a means of distribution are not ideal. Marketplaces such as Google Play and Amazon Appstore provide significant advantages, which include the following:

- Provide a review process to ensure that apps are not malicious in nature
- Provide a robust infrastructure for reaching millions of consumers and distributing apps
- Promote apps and allow consumer rating
- Handle financial settlements for purchases
- Encourage consumer trust

These advantages do come at a cost; fees paid to the marketplace and time spent in the distribution process. All of these aspects must be considered in conjunction with the goal of the app and the target audience.

Preparing for a release APK

As you may recall from *Chapter 1, The Anatomy of an Android App*, Android apps are delivered to devices for installation in an Android package format. The following sections discuss topics that should be considered prior to producing a release APK.

Disabling debug

During the development of an application, Xamarin Studio supports debugging Xamarin.Android apps through the use of **Java Debug Wire Protocol (JDWP)**. This is great for development purposes but poses security risks for deployed applications and thus needs to be disabled in released apps.

There are two different ways to accomplish this:

- Setting in `AndroidManifest.xml`
- Setting in `AssemblyInfo.cs`

AndroidManifest.xml

The following listing shows how to turn off JDWP debugging from the manifest file:

```
<application
. . .
  android:debuggable="false"
. . .
</application>
```

AssemblyInfo.cs

The following listing shows how to use a conditional directive to turn JDWP debugging off or on based on the configuration that is selected. This approach has the advantage of being based on the currently selected configuration.

```
#if RELEASE
[assembly: Application(Debuggable=false)]
#else
[assembly: Application(Debuggable=true)]
#endif
```

Linking

By default, the release mode turns off using shared runtime and turns on linking so that your distribution APK only contains the portions of Xamarin.Android runtime required by your app. The linker does this by performing a static analysis of your compiled code to determine which assemblies, types, and type members are used by your application. All unused assemblies, types, and members are discarded resulting in a significantly smaller deployable.

Linking options

Linker Options can be viewed and set in the **Project Options** dialog under the **Android Build** section:

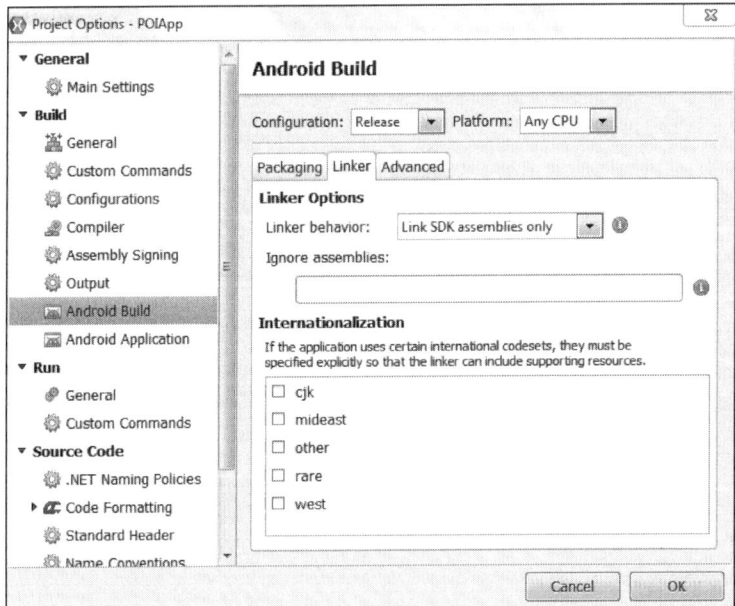

When viewing and adjusting **Linker Options**, be sure to first select **Release** from the **Configuration** drop-down box. Xamarin.Android provides the following linking behaviors:

- **Don't link**: This turns off the linker; no linking will be performed.

- **Link SDK assemblies only**: This will only link the assemblies that are required by Xamarin.Android. Other assemblies will not be linked; they will be distributed as separate assemblies.

- **Link All Assemblies**: This will link all assemblies that are required by the application and not just the ones required by Xamarin.Android.

Side effects of linking

In some cases linking can have some unintended side effects, including needed types and members being accidentally discarded. It is very important for an application compiled and linked in a release mode to be put through a thorough testing cycle in order to be certain that the app is not suffering from this side effect. In fact, in most cases, testing beyond the initial developer's testing should be conducted using an APK file and produced in the release mode.

If you encounter runtime exceptions related to missing types or trouble locating specific methods, you may need to provide a custom linker file that gives explicit instructions concerning specific types or members to the linker.

The following listing is an example of a custom linking file that directs the linker to always include a specific type and specific set of members for the type.

```xml
<?xml version="1.0" encoding="UTF-8" ?>
<linker>
  <assembly fullname="Mono.Android">
    <type fullname="Android.Widget.AdapterView" >
      <method name="GetGetAdapterHandler" />
      <method name="GetSetAdapter_Landroid_widget_Adapter_Handler" />
    </type>
  </assembly>
</linker>
```

A custom linking file can be added to a project as a simple XML file. After adding the file to the project, select the file, open the **Properties** pad, and choose **LinkDescription** for the **Build action** menu as shown in the following screenshot:

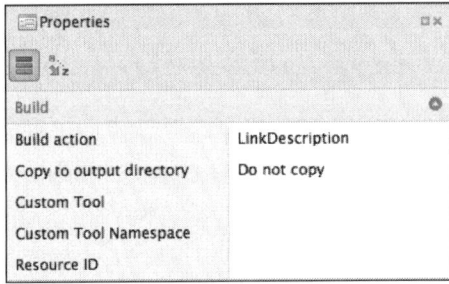

Selecting supported ABIs

Android supports several different CPU architectures. The Android platform defines a set of **Application Binary Interfaces** (**ABIs**) that correspond to different CPU architectures. By default, Xamarin.Android assumes that `armeabi-v7a` is appropriate for most circumstances. If you need to support additional architectures, you must check each that applies. This will cause the build process to generate code that will run on all the target ABIs as well as include native libraries appropriate for each architecture.

Supported ABIs can be specified in the **Project Options** dialog under the **Android Build** section:

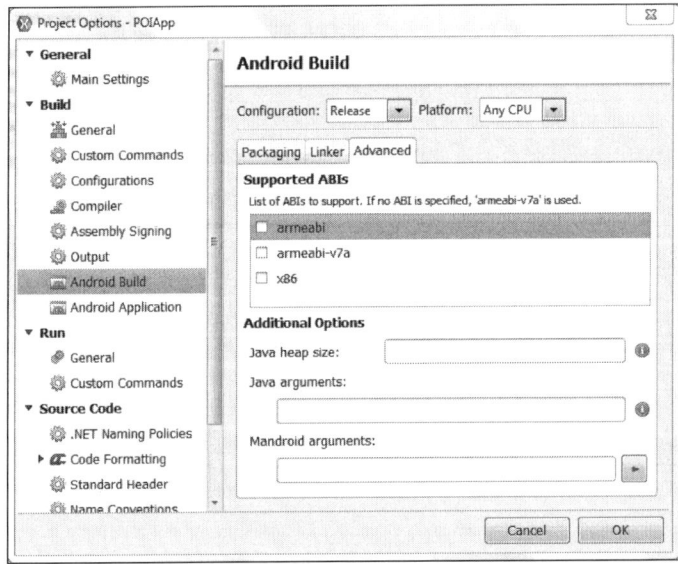

One scenario where I have run into the need of specifying additional ABIs is the testing process. I have worked with a group of testers many times, some of which have physical devices and some of which use emulators. To support the use of the x86 emulator, you will need to include x86 in the supported ABIs list.

Publishing a signed APK

Once we have made the previous decisions, we are ready to produce an APK. The following sections discuss the steps of producing a signed APK from within Xamarin Studio.

Keystores

A **keystore** is a database of security certificates created and managed by the keytool program from the Java SDK. The keystore is an important aspect of creating Android apps as the Android platform will not run apps that have not been digitally signed. This may come as some surprise, because we have been running our app for some time now. During the development process, Xamarin.Android uses a debug keystore that allows your app to run. This keystore works for debugging purposes, but will not be recognized as a valid keystore for the distribution of released apps.

While the command-line keytool program can be used directly to create and manage keystores, Xamarin.Android provides a user interface to the tool, which is integrated into the publishing process.

Publishing from Xamarin.Android

The following steps guide you through creating a new keystore as part of the process of creating a signed APK:

1. In the **Configuration** drop-down box, select **Release**:

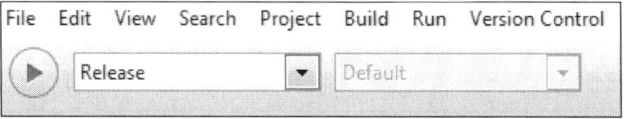

2. Navigate to **Project | Publish Android Application**; you will see the **Keystore selection** page of the **Publish Android Application** wizard as shown in the following screenshot:

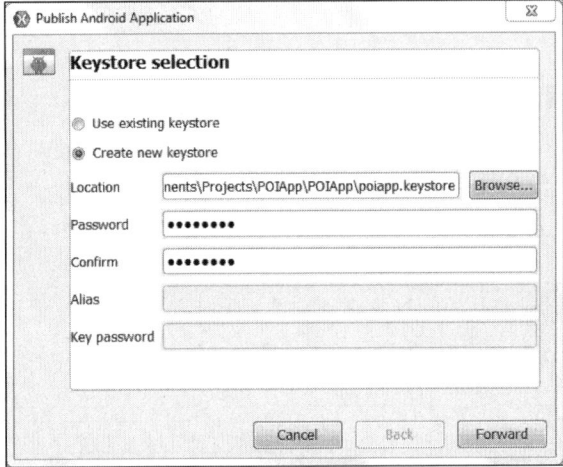

3. Select **Create new keystore**, select a location including a filename for the keystore, and enter the password and confirm it. In the example I placed the keystore in the project folder and named it `poiapp.keystore`. I just used `password` for the password.

4. Select **Forward**; you will see the **Key creation** page of the **Publish Android Application** wizard, as shown in the following screenshot:

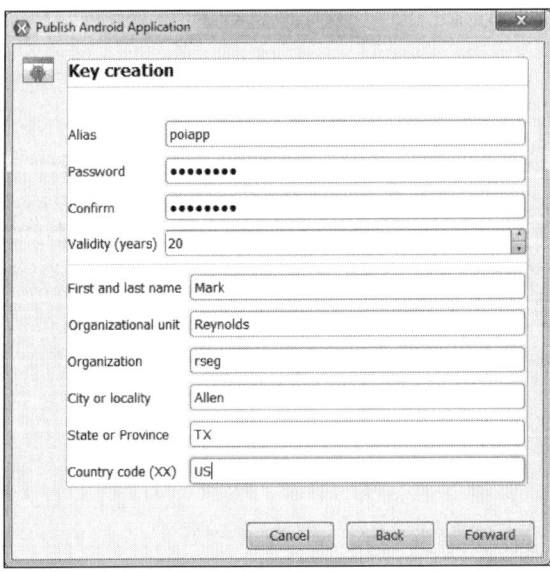

5. Enter information for all of the fields. In the example I simply used `poiapp` for the **Alias** field and `password` for the **Password** field.

6. Select **Forward**; you will see the **Select destination** page of the **Publish Android Application** wizard:

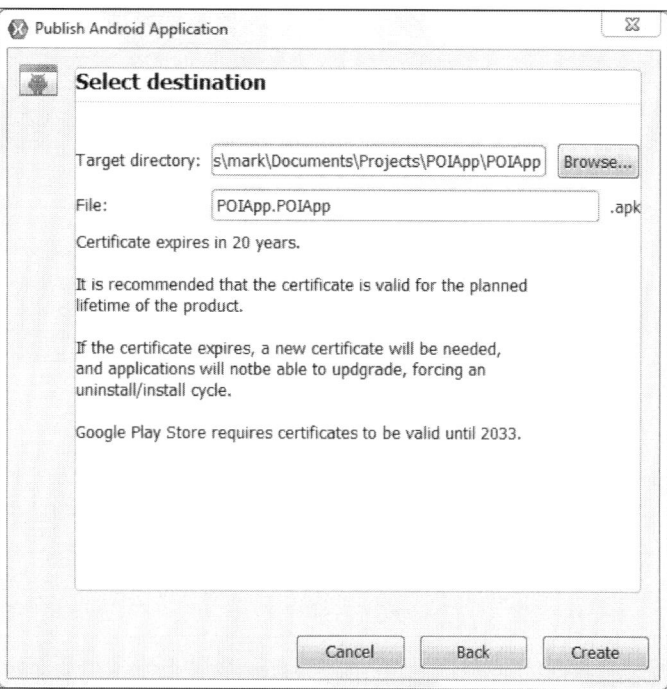

7. Select a target directory where the app will be created and click on **Create**; in this example I selected the code bundle. Xamarin Studio will compile the app for release and generate a signed APK file. You should see the following in the **Publishing package** Pad:

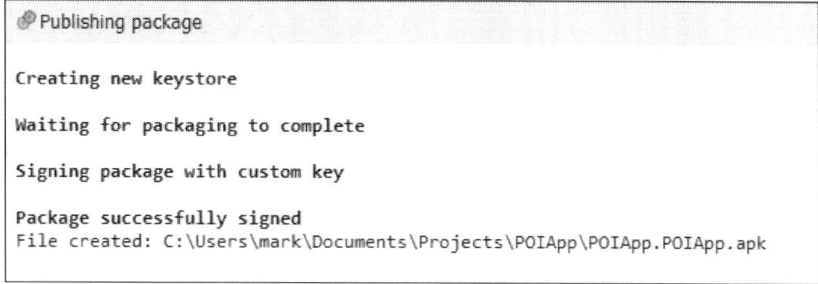

The resulting APK is ready for final testing and potential distribution. The keystore that was created is very important and should be kept and reused for subsequent deployments. The keystore, alias, and passwords should be kept secure so that only those authorized to publish a new version of the app have access to them. If a keystore is lost, it will not be possible to publish updates to an app with Google Play. The only solution would be to create a new keystore and publish the new version as a completely new app.

Republishing

As we just said, the subsequent publications of an app should use the same keystore. To accomplish this, simply select **Use existing keystore** on the **Keystore selection** page of the **Publish Android Application** wizard, locate the existing keystore, and enter the previously assigned password and alias. Refer to the following screenshot:

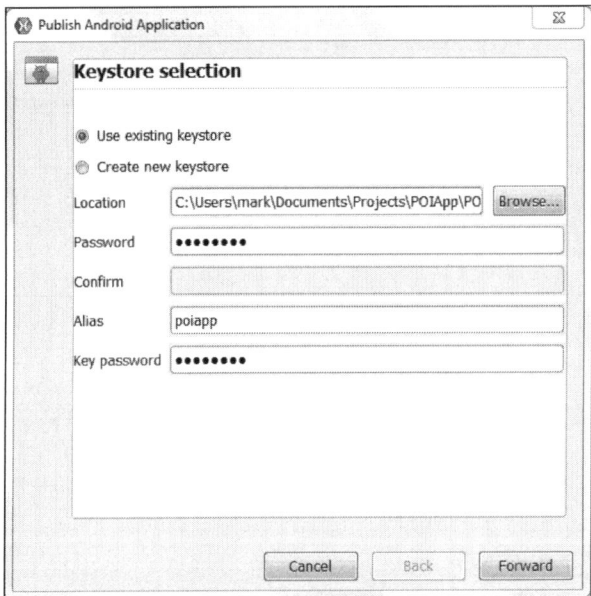

Summary

In this chapter, we have briefly discussed the options available to developers for distributing Android apps and stepped through creating a signed APK capable of being distributed.

Index

R

RefreshCache() method 61-63
registered camera apps
  checking for 128
RelativeLayout utility
  adding, to POI ListView layout 70
release APK
  debug, disabling 137
  linking 138, 139
  preparing for 137
  supported ABIs, selecting 140, 141
RequestSingleUpdate() method 108, 113
resultCode parameter 131
Reverse Geocoding 114
row clicks
  handling 84, 85
row Views
  populating 78
  reusing 78

S

sample app
  features 31
Save action
  adding 94, 95
SavePOI() method
  creating 96
  implementing 62, 63
Scale-independent Pixels (sp) 72
services 14
SetContentView() API 65
setContentView() method 18
SetEnabled() method 96
SetNegativeButton() method 100
SetPositiveButton() method 100
Setup() method 53
Show() method 116
signed APK
  keystores 141
  publishing 141
  publishing, form Xamarin.Android 141-144
  republishing 144
SimpleListItem1 layout 69
SimpleListItem2 layout 69

SQLite 47
StartActivityForResults() method 130
Success
  toasting 101

T

test methods
  Create POI test 54
  creating 54
  DeletePOI() test 56, 57
  Update POI test 55, 56
tests
  executing, Android emulator used 57, 58
  Xamarin.Android NUnitLite, setting up for 53
Text property 78
TextView classes
  adding, to POI ListView layout 72
Toast class 101
Toolbox pad 66
TwoLineListItem layout 69

U

UI elements
  adding, for image support 127, 128
UpdatePOI() method
  implementing 55, 56
UpdateUI() method 94
USB debugging
  enabling 44
USB driver
  installing 44
user
  keeping informed 116
user interface widgets
  about 15
  populating 94

V

validation
  adding 97
  EditText.Error property, using 98, 99
variables
  binding, to controls 91, 92

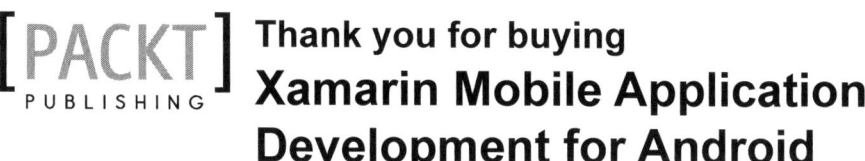

About Packt Publishing

Packt, pronounced 'packed', published its first book "*Mastering phpMyAdmin for Effective MySQL Management*" in April 2004 and subsequently continued to specialize in publishing highly focused books on specific technologies and solutions.

Our books and publications share the experiences of your fellow IT professionals in adapting and customizing today's systems, applications, and frameworks. Our solution based books give you the knowledge and power to customize the software and technologies you're using to get the job done. Packt books are more specific and less general than the IT books you have seen in the past. Our unique business model allows us to bring you more focused information, giving you more of what you need to know, and less of what you don't.

Packt is a modern, yet unique publishing company, which focuses on producing quality, cutting-edge books for communities of developers, administrators, and newbies alike. For more information, please visit our website: www.packtpub.com.

Writing for Packt

We welcome all inquiries from people who are interested in authoring. Book proposals should be sent to author@packtpub.com. If your book idea is still at an early stage and you would like to discuss it first before writing a formal book proposal, contact us; one of our commissioning editors will get in touch with you.

We're not just looking for published authors; if you have strong technical skills but no writing experience, our experienced editors can help you develop a writing career, or simply get some additional reward for your expertise.

Xamarin Mobile Application Development for iOS

ISBN: 978-1-78355-918-3   Paperback: 222 pages

If you know C# and have an iOS device, learn to use one language for multiple devices with Xamarin

1. A clear and concise look at how to create your own apps building on what you already know of C#

2. Create advanced and elegant apps by yourself

3. Ensure that the majority of your code can also be used with Android and Windows Mobile 8 devices

iOS Development Using MonoTouch Cookbook

ISBN: 978-1-84969-146-8   Paperback: 384 pages

109 simple but incredibly effective recipes for developing and deploying applications for iOS using C# and .NET

1. Detailed examples covering every aspect of iOS development using MonoTouch and C#/.NET

2. Create fully working MonoTouch projects using step-by-step instructions

3. Recipes for creating iOS applications meeting Apple's guidelines

Please check **www.PacktPub.com** for information on our titles

Printed in Great Britain
by Amazon